THE DAYDREAM
WORKBOOK

THE DAYDREAM
WORKBOOK

Learning the Art of
Decoding Your Daydreams

ROBERT LANGS, M.D.

Alliance Publishing, Inc.

ISBN 0-9641509-7-2

Book Design by Cynthia Dunne
Produced by Publisher's Studio, Albany, New York

Alliance books are available
at special discounts for bulk purchases for sales promotions,
premiums, fund-raising, or educational use.
For details, contact:

Alliance Publishing, Inc.
P.O. Box 080377
Brooklyn, New York 11208-0002

Distributed to the trade by National Book Network, Inc.

10 8 6 4 2 1 3 5 7 9

C O N T E N T S

PART I.
The Many Dimensions of Daydreams

PART II.
Daydreams in Action

PART I

The Many Dimensions of Daydreams

CHAPTER 1

The Built-in Healing Powers of Daydreams

The human mind is one of nature's most wondrous creations. There is no better evidence for these wonders than the mind's ability to imagine—to fantasize or daydream—one of its most inventive and versatile capabilities.

Ever ready to serve us, daydreams inherently possess broad curative powers. Yet they also convey messages from a remarkable unconscious intelligence, one of the most priceless endowments that nature has bestowed on us. The many uses to which we can put our daydreams staggers the very minds that create them.

By definition, a daydream is any image or scenario conjured up in your mind, however short or long. Daydreams may unfold spontaneously, without deliberate intention, or they may be designed consciously and fashioned with all due intention. They may be as varied as brief snatches or single, isolated images, or take the form of extended stories with all kinds of twists and turns. Realistic or fanciful, or mixtures of both, daydreams are the putty of the mind, ready to be shaped into countless forms from the day we first exercise our mental inventiveness and ability to tell stories to the day we are no longer able to think or imagine.

Daydreams are the unappreciated, ingenious products of human creativity. Helping you understand and make use of the many resources and benefits built into your daydreams is the main intention of this book.

The Broad Uses of Daydreams

This book will unfold as a workbook. I will ask questions and suggest exercises as we go along. This participation can be both educational and fun. The aim is to promote active learning on your part and to give you a chance to see where you stand on the topics we will be covering and the work we will be doing.

I will get us into the swing of things by asking my first question.

Question 1.1

How many uses of daydreams can you name? List them in the space provided below.

Answer 1.1

To begin with a general statement, daydreams can help us do such varied things as relax; escape from reality for a while; fulfill in fantasy all manner of hopes, aspirations, and wishes; engage in play and exercise our imaginations; solve many kinds of emotional and survival-related problems; make more effective emotional choices and decisions; resolve psychological conflicts and symptoms; enhance our relationships and interactions with others; lessen or cure our physical and emotional ills; and discover the unconscious secrets that dwell in the hearts and minds of those around us and within ourselves as well.

Few inventions of any kind, natural or man-made, are as flexible and serviceable as are our daydreams.

The scientist who imagines a solution that solves an intractable research problem, the man or woman who dreams of glories and feats beyond all human capabilities, the injured party who conjures up a tale of revenge and victory, the husband or wife who uses his or her daydreams to discover the unconscious sources of his or her conflicts and come to a peaceful resolution, the physically ill man or woman who uses positive daydreams to lessen or cure his or her illness—each, in his or her own way is tapping into the resourcefulness of daydreams.

Daydream creations are so gifted they can bring peace to us in ways that are diametrically opposite to one other. On the one hand, daydreaming is one of our most effective means of escaping from and creatively denying all kinds of painful realities and physical ills—of letting our minds at times of stress take flight into imaginary worlds of peace, health, harmony, and supernatural feats.

Yet, on the other hand, daydreams are among our finest and most reliable means of digging into and solving our everyday problems of living and coping—they can provide answers to our issues that do not materialize through frontal assaults on, and our best efforts to think through, a problem. Even more remarkably, day dreams are arguably the best means we have of gaining otherwise inaccessible yet profound insights into our emotional issues and into our world of unconscious experience—the perceptions of ourselves and others that powerfully and silently govern much of our lives. Indeed, there is no better way to work through our worst traumas and hurts than by invoking and processing our daydream responses to these disturbing events.

Daydreams are the vehicles par excellence for escape and denial, yet they serve us remarkably well for gaining the deepest insights possible into ourselves and into our emotional lives.

The very act of conjuring up a daydream, let alone working with and processing these creations towards unfathomed insights, sets our minds into action in ways that can bring us rich and surprising rewards.

Better lives through daydreaming is an apt motto for this book.

The Heritage of Daydreams

As we begin to establish the intricacies and power of daydreams, it will help to have a sense of their precursors and heritage. When we see the richness and variety of these progenitors, we will understand why daydreaming can do so much for us. Here too, let's begin with a question.

Question 1.2

What kind of activity is daydreaming? To what other activities does it bear a similarity? Which mental capabilities does it draw upon?

Answer 1.2

Daydreams have a number of interrelated sources. As a result, they belong to several different families of human expression. Mainly, the roots of daydreams are:

1.   Our capacity for language and imagery, and especially our ability to represent something in the real world by something else, and to anticipate the future and imagine events that have not occurred in the real world.

Daydreams have a variety of *representational capacities*. They may

- Directly represent or portray people and events pretty much as they were or are.
- Directly represent or portray people and events as you either wish or fear they might have been or will be in the future.
- Indirectly represent through a disguised or encoded image—a kind of symbolic or displaced or camouflaged portrayal—people or events as they have been experienced outside of awareness.

This capacity of daydreams to convey encoded messages is relatively unappreciated, but is a powerful source of otherwise inaccessible knowledge. We will develop this part of the picture slowly but surely as the book unfolds.

The first two forms of representation are straightforward—what is being portrayed is imagined directly and without disguise. A rose is a rose; a fallen tree is a fallen tree.

But the third type of representation is different. It depends on the evolved capacity of daydreams to carry two sets of meanings—one set as stated, but the other set as disguised or encoded in what has been stated. A rose is a rose, but it also is a thorny problem; a fallen tree is a fallen tree, but it also is a broken promise. One meaning is directly conveyed, while the other meaning is encoded, symbolized, if you will, in the same message.

Human language has evolved with the capacity to convey two messages at once. Our daydreams carry both direct and encoded messages.

Daydreaming is possible because, unlike other animals, the human mind is capable of representing the world in thought and images, and even more remarkably, it is able to portray the world not as it is, but as it is imagined, anticipated, wished, or feared to be. This representational function of daydreams is essential to their capacity to convey meaning. It enables daydreams to portray life problems and possible solutions, and to thereby be more than idle fantasies—daydreams have great relevance for our dealings with real problems and issues. They also have the potential to greatly enhance our ability to cope with and adapt to life's stresses and strains.

Daydreams use language and imagery to express meaning. As such, they draw on the 150,000-year-old heritage of language and of a unique ability to represent an object, person, or event in its absence. The ability to free oneself from an immediate situation and to imagine other possibilities and even other realities are among the gifts needed to daydream. So too with the gift of creating double-meaning messages mentioned earlier.

2.   *The ability to play.*

Even without language, animals engage in playful activities. Humans engage in play soon after birth and play becomes more elaborate as infants become aware of their surroundings and of other people. Playfulness expands further as soon as children have the language capability to represent the world mentally in their imagination.

Play serves many functions. It is:

- A basis for effective adaptation, growth, and development.
- A way of working over past hurts and traumas, and possible future problems as well.
- A means of developing and practicing coping and adaptive strategies and skills.
- A way of gaining pleasure from the products of our imaginations.
- A form of tension discharge—a safety valve for pent-up emotions.

Play serves us in many ways and daydreaming is the human mind at play.

3.   *The evolved capacity for mental planning and experimenting.*

Daydreams are mental forms of experimental action, ways of engaging in *thought experiments*, to borrow a term from physics. It can be very costly to test possible actions and solutions to emotional and other dilemmas in real life. Through representation, we can first experiment in our minds, thereby avoiding the detrimental consequences of misguided intentions that otherwise would prove hurtful to others and/or ourselves. Having a mental means of trying things with little in the way of real-life consequences is an invaluable capacity—and daydreams give this capacity to us as humans.

Daydreams also express and help fulfill our need to try out new ideas and gain fresh insight into ourselves and the world around us. As humans, we have a need for invention—for new ways to solve the dilemmas of the human condition and the specific issues of our everyday lives. Here too daydreams are at our service.

4.   *The human capacity and need to tell stories and dramatize aspects of life—the inclination to create narrative tales as a way of coping with life's exigencies.*

Storytelling has been with us since the beginning of mimetic expression and language. Daydreams have a deep heritage as stories or narratives whose roots lie with myths, fairy tales, plays and other forms of drama, and the like. The struggle to cope with life's ups and downs is served by daydreaming in narrative form, which facilitates the working of emotionally-charged decisions and events. In addition, narratives are the primary means through which we convey encoded messages. As such, they are critical to emotionally-charged communication.

5. *Our unique capabilities for communicating with ourselves and others in a multi-leveled fashion that embodies both conscious and unconscious, direct and disguised (encoded), meanings.*

This particular heritage, mentioned earlier, deserves special emphasis. Every story we imagine tells two tales, both related to our emotional lives. One tale is directly conveyed on the surface of a daydream and is part of our conscious thinking and world of experience. But the other tale is encoded or disguised within these same surface images and is part of our unconscious thinking and world of experience. The need for both direct and indirect, conscious and unconscious, forms of communication has been with us from the beginning of socialization and language.

Daydreams are the single most common and useful two-leveled messages created by the human mind.

6. *The human need to create, discover, grow, expand, and adapt to both life and death come together in the creation of a daydream.*

Daydreaming also draws its root from humankind's long-standing efforts to cope with life's exigencies. Humans have developed a variety of coping skills to deal with specific life events as they touch on issues related to long- and short-term survival and emotional equilibrium. The earliest human coping strategies are a notable part of the heritage of our fantasizing.

The roots of daydreaming reach back into the ancient past and are related to our basic human needs to adapt to realistic events and situations, especially events laden with emotional power. Daydreams, one of the most inventive creations of human imagination, have been fashioned to help us cope and adapt to the events of our lives. Through daydreaming, our fantasies meet reality.

This is a crucial point: Daydreams are not idle or wondrous inner fantasies detached from the realities of our daily lives. Even the most fanciful escapist daydream is a way of responding and adapting to the meaningful incidents of our lives. Whether we choose to make use of these adaptive functions or unwisely choose to ignore them, daydreams are coping responses to currently active emotionally-charged evocative or *triggering events.*

Daydreaming is a way of coping with reality.

Three Uses of Daydreams

In some vague way, most people have a sense that daydreaming can help them cope with life and bring them moments of pleasure and relief. They also have an inkling that they can learn things about themselves, and perhaps, about others, from these self-made creations. But we need a lot more than vague promises to make effective use of our daydream material. The key lies in appreciating that day dreams are not simplistic fantasies, but are rather complex and awesome structures.

A clue to the intricacies of daydreams is seen in the polarity I've already noted: Daydreams act as a means of discharging tension and bringing immediate relief on the one hand, and, on the other, as a vehicle for understanding. Notice that the relief benefits come about with no other effort than having or creating a suitable daydream. If the imagery is properly constructed with the necessary positive or escapist themes and images, the very act of daydreaming can serve you well. You needn't worry about what the daydream means, or attempt to extract insight from its contents. Dream on and be contented or healed—that's all it takes.

There's an enormous amount of meaning embodied in these storied creations. Meaning allows for learning and the development of coping skills. But learning requires effort and a sound set of guidelines for extracting the most compelling insights our daydreams can bring us.

To do this, however, we will have to go beyond the surface of our day-dreams. As I have already indicated, these mental inventions are layered with meaning—some of it out in the open, there for the taking, but much of it camouflaged or encoded within the surface imagery, so you can't see it unless you know how to undo the disguise.

While casual daydreaming for pleasure and healing may be attractive to us, we have a lot to gain from *working over or processing our daydreams toward insight*. With the sole exception of our night dreams, the pearls of deep wisdom that we discover by processing our daydreams are quite unavailable to us through any other means. Relief through discharge may work up to a point, but insight is a tool that provides us with effective solutions to our emotional dilemmas and lasting and flexible ways of adapting to present and future issues.

> *Daydreams are well qualified to be the guardians of your emotional well-being.*

In essence, then, daydreaming and daydreams can serve us in three fundamental ways:

1. As a means of *fantasizing,* which in itself has broad curative and relief-giving powers.
2. As a source of directly extractable, openly stated, or clearly implied, information and meaning—*conscious or conscious system meaning.*
3. As a source of decodable, indirectly stated, and therefore disguised or camouflaged, information and meaning—*deep unconscious or deep unconscious system meaning.*

> *Daydreams provide many avenues of comfort and remedy, and simultaneously reflect two distinctive layers of meaning. We are indeed dealing with a magnificent creation.*

Built-in Relief and Protection

As I said, the first set of benefits from daydreaming come from simply having a daydream, nothing more. I will refer to this resource as *the inherent healing capacity of daydreaming,* because these effects are built into the daydream experience; they do not require any kind of processing or understanding on the part of the daydreamer.

More than any other form of human expression, including night dreams, our daydreams have the potential to help us reduce and often cure our own malfunctions, whether in body or in mind. But even before physical or emotional problems crop up, daydreams can play a pivotal role in helping us *prevent* these malfunctions from happening at all—*they can be an essential component of an emotionally oriented, preventative, self-care program.*

Daydreaming can work both preventatively and therapeutically in both the emotional and physical realms.

On the healing side, we are gifted with a huge storehouse of resources in both body and mind, which are activated automatically at times of stress, trauma, illness, and emotionally laden concern. While all animals have similar, though far less developed capabilities, as humans we are unique in being able to extend and buttress these inborn self-curative mechanisms with elaborate, consciously orchestrated efforts to restore our mental and physical well-being when it goes awry.

Self-care of our bodies is well-known and in common practice. There is much we can do on our own to stay physically fit and well. We can, with due caution, self-treat our common colds, most of our bruises, many of our rashes, our sprained limbs, and a lot more. And, in respect to prevention, we also have a large repertoire of aids. For example, we can engage in exercise programs to support our cardiac functioning and we can take vitamin supplements to keep our bodies working in good form.

The health-ensuring capacity of daydreaming can serve our emotional well-being in a manner that is similar to the way jogging and exercising serves our physical health. All you need do is jog a couple miles three or four times each week and your cardiac status will be enhanced and your vulnerability to heart attacks reduced. You don't have to study your cardiac functioning to acquire these benefits—you just have to do the running.

In a similar manner, you don't have to understand your daydreams to benefit from exercising your imagination. However, as is true with all exercise programs, you do have to know how to properly exercise your imagination for maximum benefit. You must be aware of the kinds of stories and images that have these preventative (and healing) powers.

The Shift to Insight

Notice that, on the other hand, if your heart begins to skip beats, you will want to explore your cardiac status and discover what the skipped beats mean—understanding becomes necessary. You will, of course, be unable to carry out the investigation on your own and will need the help of a physician, but you're likely to stop jogging for a while and shift to the search for meaning and insight—and cure.

Daydreaming works in a similar fashion, in respect to your emotional difficulties. While it can provide a general lift, when the going gets rough or problems arise, you will want to shift from exercise to insight. And, in the case of emotional malfunctions, processing your daydreams makes self-diagnosis and self-cure possible. If that fails, you can and probably should go to a psychotherapist, but, within limits, there's more you can do on your own with emotional disturbances than usually is possible with a physical problem.

In-built Healing Powers

Let's focus for a moment on daydreams, for the inherent healing and prophylactic powers of these creations.

Question 1.3

Even though you attempted a general answer to the possible uses of daydreams, try now to focus on the inherent power of daydreaming in and of itself. What are the possible intrinsic benefits of daydreaming? What kinds of day dreams are most likely to have preventative and curative powers?

Answer 1.3

Daydreaming per se appears potentially to have the following beneficial effects:

1. Improvement of your general well-being.
2. Discharge of tensions.
3. Creation of a positive mood and frame of mind.
4. Release from frustrations.
5. A means of self-reassurance.
6. Escape from difficult or unbearable realities.
7. Alleviation or diminution of physical symptoms and illnesses.
8. Relief from guilt.
9. Enhancement of one's creativity.
10. Pleasure in exercising one's imagination.
11. Greater faith in your own mental capacities.

This is a rather impressive package of possible gains from an activity as natural and easy as experiencing or creating a daydream. Some experts believe you don't even have to be aware of what you have imagined, while others argue that some degree of conscious registration is necessary to benefit from your own imagination. It seems likely though that many of the beneficial effects of daydreaming will take hold whether you're aware of having had the daydream or not—as long as the contents of the daydream are of the type that promotes healing and contentment.

The Shape of Healing Daydreams

The types of daydreams that are most likely to be beneficial just by imaging their events include the following:

1. *Uplifting daydreams,* such as stories with pleasant happenings, successes, gratifications, and happy outcomes.
2. *Power daydreams,* in which the daydreamer performs great feats, defeats enemies and adversaries, gains revenge, and the like.
3. *Creative denial daydreams,* in which disasters, loss through death, injuries and illnesses, and other kinds of devastating realities are undone or obliterated from awareness.

As you can see, the emphasis is on constructive, positive, obstacle-overcoming narratives. It can be wellsaid that:

A positive daydream a day helps keep the body limber and the mind uplifted.

Exercise 1.1

Make up three positively toned daydreams. Resolve to do that each day for the next week, but feel free to make it a habit and do it regularly at some point each day from now on.

If you have a specific emotional or physical problem, use at least one of these daydreams to conjure up a story about resolving that particular difficulty. Each time you go back to the problem, imagine another solution to its ill effects, another kind of cure. If you feel down, imagine feeling up; if ill, imagine being cured and well; if frustrated, imagine ways of becoming satisfied; if hurting, picture yourself pain-free and whole again, etc.

Comment 1.1

Daydreams are one of our great healers. They are the virtual reality of our inner imagination, waiting for us to unleash their spaceless tales. The shift from potential to real imagery and themes releases the magical dust of a beneficent inner wizard. Sprinkle your daydream images around the infinite realm of your mind and hopefully live happily ever after.

Practicing the planned production of positive daydreams should be part of your daily ritual. A propitious time for positive daydreaming is at the end of the day, perhaps once you're in bed and alone mentally if not physically. But, in addition, positive daydreams can serve emergency purposes and be invoked at times of trauma or unpleasant crisis. While you will likely want to process your daydreams toward insight at such moments, creative, upbeat daydreams can be helpful until time permits a more studied approach.

With this advice, let's take a closer look at the kinds of meanings embodied in daydreams and shift to a first look at daydreaming for insight.

CHAPTER 2

And Then There Was Meaning

When most people think of daydreams, they conjure up images of escaping into a fantasy world where they feel safe and free to imagine as they will some kind of magical relief from their emotional and physical woes. We are, by natural inclination, believers in magic and generally disinclined to make an effort to understand and actively cope when something easier seems available. Because of this attitude, the use of daydreams for insight and understanding has received only passing attention and most of these efforts at comprehension are quite superficial and perfunctory. As a result, we have failed to take advantage of the remarkable endowments that nature has afforded our daydreams to communicate.

The magic of daydreaming can indeed bring moments of satisfaction and relief, some of them lasting. But, as I indicated in the first chapter, uninsightful relief is a temporary respite that cannot provide the tools needed to better cope with the next problem that arises. Daydreaming per se does not help you build adaptive resources and does not prepare you for the future. You must process your daydreams to gain fresh insights and understanding if you want to be able to better cope as life goes on.

This brings us to the second function of daydreams—their role as the carriers of information and meaning.

Two Levels of Meaning

In approaching daydreams as the carriers of meaning, we must avoid the kind of oversimplification that would restrict our understanding of the richness of these stories and their potential value. As I indicated, daydreams have been designed by evolution and natural selection to convey two messages—two sets of meanings. While some of these meanings touch on the realistic, everyday, practical problems that we are forever trying to solve, the main function of daydreams is to *carry a layering of meanings that bear upon our emotional traumas, problems, and choices.*

The essential introductory points, all of which will be developed as the book unfolds, are these:

1.   Daydreams are adaptive or coping responses and an important part of our efforts to deal with emotionally meaningful events.

2.   Daydreams are a prime vehicle for messages bearing potential insights into our emotional lives.

3.   Daydream images reveal a great deal about our perceptions of others and of ourselves, our emotional choices, and the effects of our emotionally charged experiences—so-called trigger events.

4.   These creations also contain profound insights and solutions related to our emotional concerns.

5.   Some of these adaptive solutions are conveyed directly in the surface imagery of a daydream, but the most critical coping strategies of the human mind are, oddly enough, disguised or encoded in the surface narratives of daydream creations. This means that these resources are not immediately or directly available to us—daydream images must be properly decoded to realize and use these encoded adaptive solutions.

6. The human mind is designed to cope with emotionally charged information and meaning with two basic systems—the conscious system and the deep unconscious system.

7. The conscious system is that part of the mind that is linked to awareness. Perception, experience, thinking, and processing of incoming events occur with immediate awareness or with ready and direct access to awareness. The adaptive solutions proposed by this system are arrived at through direct reasoning and are consciously fashioned and directly stated.

Conscious system thinking is reflected in the surface or manifest story of a daydream and we are able to harvest conscious insights by directly extracting meaning from these surface images.

8. The conscious system has evolved primarily to deal with and ensure immediate and long-term survival. Because so much of its energy is drained by these highly complicated and strained efforts, the system has only a very limited capacity to deal with emotional issues. Consciously, we generally respond to emotionally charged inputs with minimal understanding and with a large variety of defensive operations.

The conscious system tends to deny, obliterate, and repress many painful and anxiety-provoking aspects of emotionally charged trigger events to preserve its primary, survival-related capacities.

Another factor that renders suspect all conscious deliberations about emotional issues arises from features of the human mind that have evolved to curb human impulses toward violence. The conscious system of the mind is under the powerful influence of *unconscious guilt and need for punishment* which curtail our impulses to harm others. However, this protective device has proven to be quite costly in that it biases our conscious emotional thinking and impels us toward unwitting self-hurtful choices.

All in all, then, the conscious mind—conscious deliberations and consciously arrived at decisions—tends to be limited and often quite unhelpful or self-defeating in the emotional realm.

9. The *deep unconscious system* receives or perceives incoming stimuli—events and impressions—*subliminally and without awareness.* The system processes this incoming information and meaning—thinks through the issues and possible responses—without awareness interceding. It then *creates stories or narratives like daydreams,* through which it indicates what it has experienced, and provides a knowledgeable view of the best way to handle the issues that have been raised. These messages are, however, *always disguised or encoded;* they are never directly stated and never break through whole cloth into awareness. *Daydreams, therefore, are on this level encoded narratives that need to be properly decoded for us to benefit from the profound unconscious wisdom they contain.*

10. Where conscious wisdom is limited and often off the mark in respect to emotionally charged issues, deep unconscious wisdom is virtually always profoundly wise and on the mark. Unconsciously wrought narratives like daydreams embody *a deep unconscious wisdom* that is unavailable to us through our conscious thoughts—a way of solving emotionally related problems that is far superior to the methods available to us through direct, conscious deliberations.

   In respect to anything with an emotional element, the unconscious mind is a superior resource compared to the conscious mind.

This is why decoding the encoded and unconscious messages contained in your daydreams will enable you to make better and less hurtful emotional choices and to live a far better life than you will by limiting yourself to conscious reasoning and solutions.

11. To understand how we decode the encoded images in our daydreams, we must recall that *these creations are adaptive responses to emotionally charged trigger events.* That is, we daydream to cope with emotionally disturbing reality events and to help us bring unconscious wisdom to bear on emotionally laden decisions and choices.

   The human mind thinks through its issues both consciously and unconsciously, and unconscious thinking is revealed through decoding our daydream images.

12. Because a daydream contains encoded perceptions of the implications and meanings of trigger events and the processing of these unconsciously experienced meanings, daydream imagery and themes can be decoded only in light of these trigger events. This process is called *trigger decoding* and it is carried out by taking a given trigger event and connecting it to the daydream themes, formulating these themes as reflections of valid and sensible unconscious perceptions of the trigger event.

> *The encoded narrative of a daydream carries with it incisively accurate perceptions of the meanings of a trigger event and advice on how to deal with that event.*

In essence, then, there are two layers of meaning in every daydream, one direct and generally conscious, the other encoded and generally unconscious. Emotionally, conscious coping is defensive, limited, generally poor in its vision, and often self-defeating in its choices. On the other hand, unconscious coping is forthright, nondefensive, wise, and effective, but it cannot be directly fathomed and appreciated. To reach into deep unconscious coping you must decode the stories and themes in a daydream in light of the trigger event to which the daydream is an adaptive response.

Contrary to common belief, the deep unconscious system is not mainly a system of detached fantasies and primitive wishes. It's a system with great intelligence and wisdom in the emotional realm. Trigger decoding our daydreams enables us to benefit from that wisdom; without trigger decoding these products of our imaginations, the mind's greatest resource in the emotional domain is lost.

Trigger Decoding

While you can, of course, draw general impressions from the surface of a daydream, your insights are vastly greater and wiser when you know the emotionally charged trigger events to which your daydreams are responding. In similar fashion, decoding the themes of a daydream can lead to a general sense of meaning, but decoding these themes in light of the triggers to which they are a response provides you with precise insights as to the meanings of these encoded images.

Let's highlight two points:

- Seeing daydreams as adaptive or coping responses is essential to understanding their most vital and helpful messages and meanings.
- In thinking about the meanings of daydream images, you should use a stimulus-response model. The stimulus is a trigger event, an emotionally charged incident, while the response takes the form of direct (conscious) thoughts and actions, along with encoded narratives (reflections of unconscious processing).

A First Illustration

Let's turn to a brief example to bring home some of these vital points. Millie[1] has a daydream image of a bear suddenly coming out of the forest and hugging her, almost choking the life out of her. She frees herself and manages to get the bear into a nearby cage.

Question 2.1

What kind of daydream is this—escapist or meaning only? Explain the basis for your answer. As an exercise, take the images in Millie's daydream and turn them into a clearly escapist daydream.

Answer 2.1

Essentially, this is not an escapist dream even though the bear was put in a cage. That act is a coping response rather than a flight into

---

1.   The characters and daydreams offered in this book are presented solely for illustrative purposes. They are entirely fictitious, but are based on real experiences and are entirely sound. The inviolable requirement of total privacy and confidentiality for all persons in respect to their emotional lives precludes the use of real-life material.

positive imagery. Escapist day dreams have positive images and themes from beginning to end.

An escapist daydream might have Millie flying above the forest out of harm's way while the bear is running through the woods below her. Another possible escapist daydream would have the bear turn into a handsome man before he reaches Millie. Still another daydream could involve a peaceful interlude in the magnificence of the forest, with no bear or other threat in sight. Each of these daydreams also would have strong escapist qualities.

However, keep in mind that every escapist daydream also has meaning—both on its surface and encoded in that surface. With escapist imagery you may choose to settle for inherent relief, or you may accept that relief and then extract conscious and unconscious meanings as well.

Question 2.2
What can you say about Millie from this isolated daydream?

Answer 2.2
You can, of course, make some broad and general, tentative comments about Millie by just examining the surface of her daydream alone. For example, these images seem to suggest that Millie tends to imagine herself in dangerous situations and needs to think about how to resolve or escape them. Or you might say that Millie is trying to reassure herself that she can handle danger and threat. Perhaps she is struggling with self-hurtful or masochistic wishes and needs.

These proposals are, of course, reflections of the inner fantasy/inner need approach to daydreams. They treat daydreams as products of the imagination of the daydreamer and as part of an internal struggle to make peace with oneself. Without a view of the daydream as a response to a real event—a trigger—you can propose any number of formulations for a daydream. There is a grain of truth in most of them, but it is impossible to tell what is crucial and what is less important or even erroneous. At best, these impressions can serve as a first pass through the daydream as you head toward more definitive formulations.

Shifting your perspective to daydreaming as a way of coping with trigger events, you might propose that Millie is dealing with some kind of dangerous situation or relationship, that she's feeling smothered or trapped, or that she seems to feel that the only solution is to get rid of or incarcerate the person or animal that is evoking these feelings and anxieties in her. You could also say that Millie seems to feel endangered, but she appears to have the coping skills to deal with the danger—or wishes she did.

Without knowing the trigger event, it's impossible to distinguish wish and fantasy from reality—a real capability from a hoped-for one. But, in addition, the very nature of these statements, which are very broad and general, suggests that these kinds of impressions will not offer Millie much in the way of fresh discovery—they are unlikely to contain anything she doesn't know.

Oddly enough, because of the defensive posture of the conscious mind, we tend to think of these kinds of pronouncements as impressive and valuable—not so much despite their emptiness, but because of it. The conscious mind is attracted to pseudo-meaning as much as a moth is drawn to a flame—beware of vague generalizations when searching for meaning in daydreams. You are well advised instead to pursue specific triggers and specific meanings—encoded meanings will especially surprise you because they involve impressions you never realized.

Even if you knew a trigger event that was reflected in the manifest imagery of Millie's daydream, you would harvest only a limited amount of insight from its surface themes. Suppose Millie had been camping and a bear had approached the campsite and threatened but did not attack her. Her daydream is saying she felt trapped, that her life was endangered, and she felt that the solution to bears appearing in campsite areas is to put them all in cages.

Her surface daydream would then be a *conscious reworking* of the incident. It might well alert her to how endangered she had felt and also help her realize that she believes these animals should be put away. But, it's all rather self-evident and can be developed without the use of daydream imagery. Daydreams have more to tell us than what we already know.

To get beyond these surface considerations, as we should and must, we need to treat the daydream as an *encoded message*. Remember, the daydream is all in one both an unencoded, direct message and an encoded, camouflaged message. We are therefore simply shifting from the surface to a new level of meaning that does not negate the surface meanings of this daydream, but adds to them. It's a question of getting beyond what is self-evident and pursuing a daydream's encoded and unconscious meanings so we can deepen our understanding of the messages that these images contain.

When you turn to your daydreams in search of specific meaning and insight, you can work either of two ways: first, by starting with the daydream and then seeking out your evocative trigger events; or second, by starting with your emotionally disturbing trigger events and then turning to your daydream themes for responses and answers. Later we will develop both of these methods, but here, as an early exercise, we already have an encoded daydream so we need to find the trigger event that evoked its imagery—and to then trigger decode the themes in light of the trigger that has evoked them.

Question 2.3

Try to name at least two possible trigger events for this brief daydream. To do this, you should adopt a special way of thinking. The daydream is, on this level, a disguised response to an unmentioned trigger event. You are entering the world of unconscious experience where everything is displaced and camouflaged—encoded.

Begin your search for possible triggers by identifying the main themes in the daydream and then suggesting something that could have evoked that kind of imagery. A good way to do this is to take the main themes in the daydream imagery and identify their most general meanings, and then think of something that could have happened that has attributes that involve comparable themes. Triggers and themes are like locks and keys—they are two aspects of the same experience.

Answer 2.3

The main themes are animal, suddenly coming out of somewhere, hug, crush, possible loss of life, entrapment, freeing oneself, caging an animal, and being able to handle a dangerous situation.

The question we must ask now is this: What kind of experiences contain these very qualities that would be capable of evoking these themes? The central images involve danger, entrapment, and response by imprisonment. The trigger event could be any specific event that felt entrapping to Millie—a job, a class at school, or a relationship.

For example, Millie's widowed mother might have been ill and could have insisted Millie not go on vacation because she needed her daughter to care for her. Here, the themes shared by the trigger and the daydream images are those of entrapment and imprisonment.

Or, the man Millie was living with could have acted in a smothering and entrapping way, as for example, by insisting on having sex with her when she didn't want to.

The actual trigger event in this case was, however, a pass that Millie's boss had made at her, which Millie *consciously* reacted to with mixed feelings. The boss was an attractive but married man who claimed he was going to leave his wife. Millie vacillated between deciding to stay clear of him and thinking of ways to encourage him to pursue her. In typical conscious system fashion, she couldn't make up her mind about what to do, although she was inclined to keep the seduction going.

In contrast, her deep unconscious mind was quite clear in its view of the trigger event with the boss. Unconsciously, Millie had perceived and processed the incident as entirely assaultive and entrapping—and quite dangerous. Where her conscious intelligence waffled and leaned toward further involvement with the boss, her deep unconscious intelligence was warning Millie to steer clear of the man—he was dangerous. It also was recommending some kind of punishment and restraint for the boss, in the image of putting the bear in a cage.

The differences between conscious and unconscious appraisals of the same situation are evident here. Millie's conscious view and inclinations have self-destructive elements in that the boss had used this tactic with other women employees with whom he had brief affairs that ended with a lot of turmoil and hurt—incidents Millie had consciously repressed for the moment. As I said, this kind of self-defeating obtuseness and poor judgment is typical of the conscious mind—all the more wondrous that we ever make constructive choices when emotions are involved.

Conversely, Millie's deep unconscious intelligence sees the situation and her boss for what they are, understands the dangers Millie is facing, and recommends an effective, adaptive solution—get rid of the man.

We see again then that:

1. The deep unconscious mind is exquisitely in touch with emotionally charged realities, while the conscious mind tends to be out of touch with many aspects of reality.
2. Using our daydreams to obtain conscious system insights is quite limited and very risky in that our conscious needs are unconsciously governed by unrecognized self-punitive needs.
3. Using trigger decoding to get in touch with your unconscious responses to trigger events is a most necessary pursuit if you want to understand yourself and others, and want to discover the best and least punitive solutions to your emotionally charged concerns.

Trigger decoding your daydreams taps into the most profound wisdom the human mind can presently generate, wisdom the mind conceals from itself and reveals only through disguised images. Trigger decoding enables us to cope with life's exigencies in the best ways possible.

We have a sense now of the three ways daydreams can serve us. Clearly, their revelations, in light of triggers, as they enable us to develop our adaptive resources, are the most compelling aspect of these creations. Because meaning is so critical to the optimal use of daydreams, and because encoded meaning is generally an unfamiliar topic, let's pursue this aspect of daydreams further in the next chapter.

CHAPTER 3

Meaning and Healing

e've had a first look at the inherent healing powers of daydreaming. In this chapter, we extend our pursuit of meaning in daydreams by turning to ways in which understanding our daydreams can provide us with even more powerful means of healing our physical and emotional ills, while informing the rest of our emotional lives.

Other than going to a psychotherapist, most people have only the vaguest idea about how they might help themselves resolve an emotional dilemma or even alleviate some of the more common emotional symptoms like bouts of depression or anxiety. Effective ways of curing our own emotional ills and restoring our mental health seem to have eluded us even though a large part of the answer has been with us for thousands of years in the form of our night and daydreams. As we saw, their use for insight is ours for the asking—we just need to know how to ask.

Using our daydreams for understanding also can be a valuable way of exercising our minds. We are engaged in some form of daydreaming during approximately half of our waking hours and we can conjure up more daydreams on demand. By processing our daydream stories we can improve our abilities to use our minds to understand our emotional selves, and we actually can prevent emotional disturbance and better solve our emotional problems for having done so.

Daydreaming is the mind's way of giving us an opportunity to actively prevent and heal emotional malfunctions through insight and understanding.

Resolving Emotional Difficulties

If you experience an emotional problem like a phobia or a noticeable depression, or recurrent issues in relating to others, you probably have no precise idea about how you might resolve the difficulty on your own. As you may have noticed, the basis for an emotional difficulty cannot simply be recognized directly, talked out, and then resolved. As Freud taught us, these difficulties have both conscious and unconscious sources, and by definition, the unconscious roots of an emotional problem cannot reach awareness directly in a straightforward manner. To be emotionally stable and happy, we need something more than a frank, direct approach.

Because of these unconscious roots, you seldom can talk yourself out of an emotional problem. But you can accomplish a great deal by processing your daydreams and getting to the unconscious sources of whatever is bothering you at the moment.

Processing your daydreams is a superb means of getting to the powerful unconscious sources of an emotional disturbance.

Processing our daydreams also is a way of improving our emotional I.Q—our psychological coping capabilities. Just as we can learn more effective ways of dealing with the real world and study to improve our social and survival skills, we also can learn how to decode our daydreams to improve our skills in dealing with the world of emotionally charged human experience.

Question 3.1
In principle, what are some of the ways processing your daydreams can help you alleviate an emotional difficulty, to function better, and have a more satisfying life?

Answer 3.1

Broadly speaking, daydreams can be used insightfully for healing by helping you:

- Consciously sort out and think things through.
- Return to your earlier years to discover the genetic roots of a current problem.
- Tap into your unconscious thoughts and adaptive solutions.
- Use these various avenues of insight to resolve a specific emotional problem.

The Uses of Processing Your Daydreams

To be more specific, we are dealing with two levels of insight—those derived from determining the *conscious meanings* of the surface images of a daydream and those found through the trigger decoding of the *unconscious meanings* disguised in these same images. In reworking these two levels of understanding, we soon learn to afford decoded insights the main say in solving our emotional issues. On this basis, the insights and understanding derived from processing your daydreams can be used to:

1. Find solutions to current or anticipated problems, especially aspects of your emotional life that are in need of healing, and for improving your skills at doing so.
2. Rework past traumas and incidents to minimize their harmful effects.
3. Enhance your creativity by developing and gathering new ideas and inventions that your daydreams reflect, including those encoded in their images.
4. Enter the distinctive, inventive, bold world of unconscious experience by means of trigger decoding your daydream images. Thinking in terms of unconscious experience is inherently creative and is certain to widen your horizons and enhance your coping skills.

5. Counter the tendency of the conscious mind to arrive at poor solutions to emotional problems and choices, and lessen the influence of unconscious guilt on emotionally laden decisions.

6. Reduce and even alleviate emotional disturbances and some physical disorders, and, as noted, reduce or prevent their occurrence.

7. Understand yourself, others with whom you interact, and the events of your life in terms of your specific responses to particular emotionally charged experiences.

8. Improve your general coping skills so you are better prepared for future incidents.

9. Test and explore possible life changes—work-related, relationships, family ties, geographic, career, etc. As products of your imagination, with minimal effects on others or yourself in the interpersonal/interactional world, daydreams are an excellent means of trying out new ideas, planning life changes, and imagining various possibilities and their likely consequences— of engaging in thought experiments rather than enacting all sorts of potentially disruptive scenarios. It is, however, especially important, in processing these *anticipated imagined trigger events,* to be certain to not only explore the surface meanings of your responsive daydreams, but to trigger decode their themes in light of the expected situation—unconscious insights are an invaluable aid.

10. Enhance your ability to handle yourself in stressful situations and in relation to others.

11. Understand your needs and wishes, your sexual and aggressive feelings and impulses, and your conflicts and identity issues.

12. Motivate yourself to take adaptive action in the face of adaptive challenges.

13. Manage your emotional life and its exigencies.

Processing your daydreams is a gifted means of finding new ways of being more creative and better adapted, and having a more fulfilling life.

Daydreams and Meaning: An Illustration

Let's consider another brief example. Barbara is a young woman who teaches European history in a high school. Between classes she has a daydream that she's being given the teacher-of-the-year award at the annual meeting of her school district. She wins the award because of a very favorable poll conducted by the student body and because she has just published a book entitled *Medical Practices in Europe During the Dark Ages.*

Here is another daydream. Before we get to the problem—*the trigger event*—that it deals with, let's answer a few basic questions about its surface imagery.

Question 3.2

What type of daydream is this—escapist or meaning only? Explain your answer.

Answer 3.2

This daydream has a very positive set of images and as such, it qualifies as an escapist daydream. However, the conscious mind's penchant for defense and flight is such you can assume that any spontaneous daydream with entirely positive imagery is, in addition to its upbeat features, an attempt to cope with some kind of stress through avoidance and denial. This function does not, however, detract from the inherent healing qualities of simply having a daydream of this kind—it simply adds another dimension to the situation.

In any case, by virtue of having conjured up this brief and highly favorable narrative, Barbara experienced an immediate sense of exhilaration—for the moment, she had escaped the traumas and stresses she was dealing with. Her daydream had given her a brief moment of *healing without meaning.*

In principle, however, every daydream, even those of an escapist and highly positive nature, is a response to an emotionally charged trigger event—a psychological trauma. Daydreams are by no means merely idle fantasies or moments of pause and relief divorced from the emotional issues that concern us each day.

Indeed, an entirely hopeful, positive daydream is often indicative of a major underlying, traumatic trigger event.

Question 3.3

We still are without the trigger event that evoked this daydream story. Nevertheless, as a preliminary probe, what can you say about Barbara and her life situation by looking at her daydream alone?

Answer 3.3

A positive daydream actually tells you very little about the daydreamer. It is, of course, possible that the daydream is a replay of an actual event, which would render it rather innocuous. However, this happens not to be the case here. Perhaps the best we can say is Barbara appears to be an optimistic person who either values herself highly or has high aspirations. There's a hollowness to this kind of simplistic thinking for two reasons: first, it's all too self-evident, and second, it's very likely that her elevating daydream is, as I said, a reaction to a significant traumatic trigger event. In addition, without the trigger, we have no way of knowing if the daydream is sheer fantasy or a reflection of real events.

We are at a great disadvantage when we try to understand a daydream and its dreamer without knowledge of his or her immediate triggers—the adaptive issues with which the daydream is dealing. Meaning in daydreams, even when it is directly stated, implies coping, and coping implies dealing with something, and dealing with something in the emotional realm implies the existence of some kind of stressful event.

*Daydreaming is part of our efforts to adapt to stress—
to traumatic trigger events.*

Finally, let's put this daydream into its context and define the problem Barbara was trying to solve at the time of her fantasy. The stressful trigger event was that Barbara had been told earlier that day that her department chairperson, a man named Ed, was arranging to have her transferred next semester to another school. His stated reason for the move was that the other school needed Barbara more than he did.

Questions 3.4

Now that we know one of the evocative trigger events for this daydream, we can ask several questions. Is the trigger event alluded to directly in the daydream? If so, how? If not, is it somehow disguised or encoded in the daydream, and if it is, how is that disguise accomplished? Also, what coping strategy or response to the anticipated trigger event is reflected on the surface of the daydream images?

Answers 3.4

The trigger event is not mentioned directly in the daydream. Instead, it obtains a *disguised or encoded representation* in the fact that the daydream is about Barbara's position as a teacher. The *bridging themes*, which connect and are shared by the daydream and the trigger event, are *teaching and school*. This is representation by displacement, allusions to the setting without mention of the specific evocative trigger. The disguise is minimal. A daydream about being sent to boarding school as an adolescent is an example of a more disguised representation of this trigger event.

Several important points follow from these observations:

1. The critical trigger events for many daydreams are not alluded to directly in the daydream story. However, in almost all instances where this occurs, there is an *encoded representation*

or disguised allusion to the relevant incident. This means that even when you are searching for the meaning and coping strategies reflected in the surface or manifest contents of a daydream, you will find it necessary to *seek out triggers not alluded to directly in the daydream story.* This search can be carried out by looking for your most significant recent stress situations or by turning to the daydream itself to find encoded clues to the trigger events at issue.

2. A key point is that in many important instances, the critical experiences you are trying to cope with are not referred to in the surface daydream that you've generated as part of these coping efforts.

You cannot extract direct or encoded meaning from a daydream without knowing its evocative trigger.

3. In this respect, the are two types of daydreams:
   • Those in which the significant trigger events for the daydream are referred to directly in the daydream itself.
   • Those in which the significant trigger events for the daydream are referred to in encoded fashion through one or more disguised images.

In the first type of daydream, the conscious response and manifest imagery usually are self-evident. However, there is always another trigger event encoded in the same daydream images and the daydream itself is a response to both the manifest and encoded trigger experiences.

For example, Mark, a college student, fails calculus. On the day he receives his grade, he has a daydream of taking a make-up examination and getting an A on it. His images shift and he next sees himself attacking his calculus teacher by choking him until he collapses to the floor.

In both of these brief narratives, the daydream manifestly alludes to the trigger event. However, because every daydream deals with several triggers at once, there are, as I said, other triggers for Mark's daydream that are not alluded to directly—they are encoded in the images. For example, Mark was also dealing with a fainting episode that his mother had suffered. That particular trigger event, which

Mark had repressed for the moment, is encoded in the allusion of the teacher falling to the floor.

We can now add three more principles to our list:

1. Every daydream is layered with meaning and is a response to two or more trigger events.
2. For each daydream we have, some of the triggers may be alluded to directly, but others will be encoded in the images.
3. Daydreams are not simply reflections of human personalities and viewpoints frozen in space and time. They are, instead, reflections of human personalities and viewpoints as activated by real trigger events.

Returning to Barbara, in light of her trigger event, we can now define the coping strategy reflected in her daydream. Barbara's daydream places her in an almost unassailable position in which transfer would be unthinkable. She imagines herself as very well thought of by her students, and as having published her book and receiving a coveted award.

To formulate the adaptive meaning of the surface of a daydream in light of its trigger, we should construct a story of adaptation that begins with the stimulus (trigger) and ends with the response (the decoded themes). Here, the tale would run like this: You (Ed) want to get rid of me, but I am so popular, so effective, and so well published that you dare not do it.

Outside of her daydream, in her direct, conscious responses to this anticipated trigger, Barbara felt helpless and at a loss about what she could do to keep her position at her present school—which is what she wanted consciously. But daydreaming draws upon another level, that of unconscious thinking, one that is richer in its resourcefulness than our direct thoughts about a situation.

In this instance, Barbara is simply defeated in thinking through what she might do in responses to Ed's plan. But her daydream images do not lack ideas; they propose a number of adaptive suggestions—ways that Barbara might get Ed's decision reversed. This is another important reason to daydream and link images to their triggers.

Conscious deliberation and direct efforts to cope with emotional triggers vary, depending on whether you make a frontal attack on the problem or deal with it indirectly through a daydream. In general, daydreaming intelligence is superior to the intelligence reflected in trying to cope directly with your emotional issues.

You can see then that much is to be gained by allowing a free flowing daydream to materialize when dealing with emotional triggers— and then processing the daydream for the answers it contains. Even on the conscious level, the solutions to emotional issues that we arrive at through direct deliberation are different from those we arrive at by turning away from the problem, creating a daydream, and then deriving the solutions revealed by its images and themes. To these insights you can add the further solutions advocated in the encoded themes discovered through trigger decoding, thereby producing a powerful package of adaptive wisdom. You're likely to do very well using this kind of multi-leveled knowledge base for dealing with your emotional concerns.

Three Levels of Wisdom

In coping with emotionally charged trigger events—stresses and traumas—the human mind has three levels of intelligence and coping skills:

1. Conscious wisdom that operates by means of direct reasoning and deliberation concerning the issue at hand. This is our *direct coping conscious intelligence.*
2. Conscious wisdom that is revealed through images conjured up in the course of daydreaming without confronting the problem directly. This is our *indirect coping conscious intelligence.*
3. Deep unconscious wisdom that is expressed through encoded images in daydreams and revealed only through trigger decoding. This is our *unconscious coping intelligence.*

Barbara's daydream can be translated into real-life coping strategies. The images advise her to enhance her popularity with her students and to make that popularity known to Ed and others. They also tell her to get moving on the book she is writing and to try to promote herself for the teacher-of-the-year award, for which she is in the running.

Daydream images always translate into coping strategies, many of them unavailable to us when thinking things through directly as they pertain to specific trigger events.

Unconscious Coping Strategies

We have identified the *conscious* coping suggestions reflected in Barbara's daydream. We now want to discover her *unconscious* coping recommendations as well. To determine what they are we need to know at least one of Barbara's associations to her daydream. As we will see, the most compelling meanings of daydream images can be accessed only by generating (associating) fresh stories that are brought to mind by the surface elements of the daydream story.

The award ceremony evoked in Barbara's mind the awards given at last year's annual meeting of the school district. There had been one disturbing note connected with that occasion. The man who had received the award for developing the most creative course curriculum for his classes was accused a week later of trying to seduce a student who had rebuffed his advances, and against whom he had then taken punitive actions.

Question 3.5

Even without knowing the details of trigger decoding, can you tie Barbara's anticipated trigger event to this story and its themes? Try to do a readout of Barbara's likely unconscious perceptions of the trigger situation—of Ed in particular—as encoded in this associated story. To develop the answer, lift the themes of the story from its surface context and place them into the trigger situation. See what you can do.

Answer 3.5

Barbara's unconscious reaction to the trigger event as encoded or displaced and disguised in this story seems to read like this: You (Ed) are considered such an innovative chairperson, but the real reason you want to transfer me is that you've been trying to seduce me and I've been rebuffing your advances; you want to punish me for doing that.

As you can see, to trigger decode this associated story, we extract its themes and simply place them into the trigger situation, reading out the result as a real perception. This readout is based not so much on Barbara's conscious experience of her relationship with her chairperson, but on her *unconscious perceptions* of what had been going on. We are dealing with the striking differences between conscious and unconscious experience—one is rather blocked and the other remarkably open.

On the surface, Barbara thought of Ed as a bit too friendly, but his seductive intentions had not registered in her awareness of the situation. Barbara was by nature rather standoffish; she had not been deliberately putting off Ed. Still, her deep intelligence was telling her what was going on—and it happened to be right on the mark.

> *Unconscious perception always is more in touch with reality than conscious perception.*

Validating this impression with additional encoded associations would give Barbara confidence that this was the issue motivating Ed's decision to send her elsewhere. It also would enable Barbara to deal with Ed in a completely different way than she would have, based on her conscious reading of the situation. While she would be well-advised to not suddenly confront Ed with this issue—he would only deny everything—she could more subtly and carefully approach this underlying problem in a way that would allow them to rework it and hopefully resolve the issues involved. In any case, she would now be able to develop a coping strategy that took this consciously unnoticed, but unconsciously perceived, aspect of the situation into account.

Some Useful Principles

Notice the following:

1. Conscious appraisals of stressful trigger situations tend to be self-evident, naive, and superficial; they seldom take into account the underlying and more powerful aspects of the situation.
2. Deep unconscious appraisals of the same situation tap into repressed and powerful aspects of what is going on—aspects that entirely escape direct awareness.
3. Your coping strategy will move in one direction if it is based solely on conscious thinking. It will, however, move in a very different and more effective direction if unconscious thinking is brought into play.
4. The best solutions to an emotionally charged trigger event come from combining conscious and unconscious perceptions and recommendations for coping—and relying mostly on your unconscious view of the situation.

Using daydreams for escape and mood elevation comes easy. Using these same creations to access meaning and to discover effective and lasting solutions to your emotional concerns takes work. But the rewards for the effort are enormous. Much of what is healthy and truly beneficial in this life comes only with devoted concentration. This is certainly true when it comes to learning how to best deal with your emotionally charged triggers—the essence of your life.

Daydreams are the mind's own gift of wisdom to itself and to the owner of that mind. A large part of that gift comes wrapped in camouflage. It's well worth the effort to unwrap this gift, as it contains the secrets to a happy and productive life.

Daydreams and Night Dreams

Daydreaming is the human mind at play; it is the mind in action, the mind exploiting its greatest gifts—language and imagery; it is the mind at work, solving problems and healing itself, consciously and unconsciously; it is the mind coping with life's exigencies and the mind at its height of creativity. Quite a package, yet so unappreciated. Let's look at why this is so.

Question 4.1

Given the importance and value of daydreams, can you think of some reasons why so few people appreciate what daydreams have to offer us and why even fewer people make it routine to process their daydreams on a daily basis?

Answer 4.1

There are many reasons why we have failed to properly value our daydream stories and their inexhaustive potential. Note the following:

1. Spontaneous daydreams often go unnoticed and therefore unprocessed and unappreciated.

2. There is a tendency to think that because daydreams are products of our imaginations, they are merely fantasy formations, expressions of wishes and reflections of our personalities. We tend to treat these tales as if they were quite divorced from the realities of our everyday lives, which is, of course, not the case at all. Daydreams are mistakenly thought of as respites from life rather than part of the very fabric of our existence. Still, the idea that daydreams belong to our imaginations and not to the real world undermines our respect for these creations.

3. We have so greatly emphasized the use of daydreams as a means of escaping reality and unleashing our imaginations that we have failed to realize that these creations are deeply meaningful and profoundly useful in other important ways.

4. Similarly, we have adopted such a simplistic view of daydreams that they have been devalued in our eyes. We tend to think of these creations as straightforward efforts to rework old problems and traumatic events, and as rather direct ways of anticipating future incidents. In all, we have missed the great complexity of daydreams, and with that, their deeper powers and wider application to the events of our lives.

5. We also have not learned much about how daydreams can and should be worked over and processed to generate genuinely new personal insights that help us cope with life's exigencies. This is especially true of the encoded aspects of daydream imagery, which actually reflect the most compelling and unforeseen aspects of daydream messages.

6. Daydreams are stories—narratives. And, as I have indicated, narratives are carriers of both conscious and unconscious meaning. Because unconscious meanings touch on extremely fearful aspects of ourselves and others, every vehicle of unconscious expression is perceived as dangerous—even though the meanings they contain are disguised or encoded. It is, then, our dread of consciously realizing our own unconscious expe-

riences that contribute to our neglect of daydreams—especially in respect to their trigger decoded messages.

In simple terms, the fear of the unconscious aspects of our lives leads us to depreciate the daydreams that are in touch with that particular dimension of human experience.

7. Finally, our undying fascination with *sleep or so-called night dreams* and our beliefs in their magical powers has blinded us to the realization that daydreams are every bit as magical and valuable as their nighttime counterparts. In fact, daydreams are more versatile and serviceable than night dreams—a contention I will now elaborate on so as to afford daydreams their rightful place in our thinking and our ways of coping in the emotional world.

Comparing Daydreams and Night Dreams

We want now to compare the nature and structure of daydreams and night dreams.[1] I will begin by asking a question.

Question 4.2

List all the similarities and differences between daydreams and night dreams that occur to you. Overall, how similar and different do you think these two products of our imaginations are—more alike than different, or more different than alike? Indicate why you think as you do.

---

1.   I will refer to dreams experienced during sleep as *dreams, night dreams* (even though people also sleep during the day), and *sleep dreams*, while I will allude to the products of our waking imaginations, primarily expressed via private mental scenarios, as *daydreams, waking dreams, fantasies*, and *conscious fantasies*. In essence, one type of imagination is expressed during sleep, the other while awake.

Answer 4.2

Thanks to their occurrence during the altered state of consciousness that is sleep—which contributes to their enigmatic qualities, frequent sense of unreality, strangeness, and other unusual attributes—*night or sleep dreams* rather than *day or waking dreams* have been the main attraction for most people who are interested in the mysteries of *the emotion-related or emotion processing mind.* Freud set the pattern in 1900 in his landmark book, *The Interpretation of Dreams,* by selecting dreams as his model of unconscious expression; Jung largely followed suit.

As a result, we tend to place dreams in a special, somewhat magical place, apart from other forms of communication, and to put daydreams in that other group of more ordinary ways of expressing ourselves. Thus, there has been a tendency to stress the differences between these two fantasy productions and to ignore or minimize their many similarities.

Over the years, a burgeoning number of books have been written about dreams, from a wide variety of viewpoints. The emphasis is on their deep meanings and healing powers and the seemingly supernatural capabilities of the dreaming mind. The fact that daydreams occur when we are awake, as well as the smaller body of writings on this subject and the failure to notice the communicative capabilities and powers of daydreams, all contribute to making them seem far different from, and less important than, night dreams. The overall attitudes toward these two types of dream formations favor differences over similarities, night dreams over daydreams.

Another problem arises from the tendency of many people to view both daydreams and night dreams as fantasy creations relatively divorced from immediate realities—a proposed feature that I have already questioned. Nevertheless, many writers currently suggest that in some global and ill-defined way, our night dreams actually do inform our reality issues, but they seldom suggest that the same is true of daydreams—which is, of course, the case as well.

The differences between daydreams and night dreams also are emphasized through an erroneous tendency to stress the phantasmagoric and unreal qualities of dreams, and to contrast these features with daydreams, which are believed to involve images that tend to be far more realistic. While there are indeed many daydreams that tell stories that reflect and rehearse real happenings (as do some sleep dreams), many of our daydreams are as unrealistic as the wildest of our night dreams. We readily daydream of monsters, supernatural feats, the undoing of the death of loved ones, and an endless variety of impossible happenings.

The similarity between daydreams and night dreams in this regard is brought home when you afford daydreams their widest possible definition. On this basis, *daydreams include all of our waking acts of creativity such as novels, plays, and movies.* A quick review of the latest movie fare will help you realize that the two worlds of imagination—daydreams and night dreams—are very similar indeed. Genies, vampires, blood-sucking monsters, murders, time machines, bizarre physical images, strange happenings, and many other kinds of images that defy reality populate these art forms. They embody as much of the strange and impossible as any collection of sleep dreams we can muster.

We have but one imagination and one capacity to develop encoded narratives which can operate by day or night, while we are asleep or awake.

Similarities and Differences

We can now list the similarities and differences between daydreams and night dreams based on a general understanding of the two types of expression. This initial list of general features will later be supplemented by a list that takes into account their deeper structures as well. As for *differences:*

1. Dreams occur during sleep, daydreams while we are awake.
2. Dreams occur spontaneously without conscious control, while daydreams can be consciously fashioned and controlled. The exception to this difference lies with lucid dreams, in which the sleep dream is consciously modified by the creation of a waking dream state in which the dreamer controls and manipulates his

or her dream imagery. Indeed, a lucid dream is a combination of a night and daydream, showing that the two can be blended—a point that leads to a similarity rather than a difference.

3. Night dreams tend to be more fragmented and disconnected in their sequences of images than do daydreams. However, daydreams can shift about illogically and unrealistically in ways similar to night dreams, so there is similarity here as well.

4. There is some sense that night dreams conjure up more forgotten or repressed memories in their surface contents than do daydreams. However, I know of no test of this idea, and daydreams often have elements of repressed memories in them as well. As we will see, both forms of imagination frequently embody encoded versions of repressed memories, and are somewhat similar in that respect.

We can see then that there appears to be few significant differences between night and daydreams. The commonly held belief that night dreams are far more unrealistic than daydreams has already been addressed and essentially refuted. Before drawing some conclusions, however, let's make our second list.

Daydreams and night dreams are *similar* in the following ways:

1. Both are usually experienced in the form of narratives and images, most often visual in nature, though occasionally using other senses like hearing, touch, and smell.

2. In their recounting, both are described through language shaped into storied form.

3. Both can be realistic or entirely unrealistic.

4. Both come from our imagination.

5. Either form can directly rework a realistic or emotional problem, though daydreams tend to accomplish this more than night dreams.

All things considered, it appears that *daydreams and night dreams are far more similar than different.* An appreciation of their deeper structures (both carry two messages) and their adaptive functions (both are designed to cope with emotional realities) fully supports this contention.

The Structure of Narrative Forms

To appreciate the extent to which daydreams and night dreams are similar, we should take a closer look at human language and its capacity to convey two different messages in a single story line. The discovery that this capacity is a property of all narrative tales was crucial to the realization that as narratives, daydreams and night dreams have similar structures.

As we have seen, every story conveys a surface or manifest tale that ultimately is related to one or more emotionally charged trigger events. At the same time, the story conveys a camouflaged or encoded tale that also is related to important trigger events. Sometimes, the surface and encoded messages deal with the same trigger event and present two rather distinctive views of that experience. But quite often, the surface meanings of a daydream deal with one trigger, while the encoded meanings deal with a different trigger event. Furthermore, as we will see, the coping responses to trigger events reflected in the surface imagery of a daydream tend to be broad and varied in their scope, while the coping responses to trigger events reflected in the encoded imagery tend to be concentrated on issues of rules and boundaries—frames and contexts.

As narratives, however, these vital surface and encoded properties pertain to both daydreams and night dreams.

A Case in Point

Donald, a married accountant in his late 30s, wakes up one morning and remembers a dream fragment in which he is a passenger in a car that is in an accident. He's trapped in the car, but suddenly finds himself in an operating room about to have his leg amputated. He gets up from the operating table and walks away, pointing out that his leg has already healed itself.

Donald wakes from the dream feeling anxious, makes note of what he dreamt, and goes about his daily business. He senses there were other dreams, but he's unable to recover them.

During an afternoon coffee break, Donald has a daydream in which he's at his dentist's office and is sitting in the dentist's chair about to have a tooth pulled. As the dentist starts to administer the anesthesia gas, Donald's body becomes lighter and lighter and he floats out of the office, commenting to the dentist as he leaves that his tooth is fine.

Question 4.3

Let's begin our exploration of the similarities and differences between daydreams and night dreams by looking at the surface of these two stories—one a sleep dream, the other a daydream. What similarities, if any, do you see? What differences, if any?

Answer 4.3

If we look first at the form of these two creations, we see they both are, as expected, narratives or stories. Each has elements that are possible in reality, but each also has an element that is not. The dream has an impossible sudden change in scene, while the daydream has an unrealistic feat—floating away from the dentist's office.

In terms of content, the dream is about a car accident and leg amputation, while the daydream is about having a tooth pulled. Given these manifest differences, we nonetheless can appreciate that the core of each story involves the threatened loss of a body part—a leg in one story, a tooth in the other.

All in all, the surface of these two creative expressions seems far more similar than different—especially in respect to their basic structures.

The Search for Meaning

Ultimately, we want to fully understand the meanings of these two dream-form narratives. Many people would be inclined to abstract the surface of these narratives and propose that Donald must be suffering from some kind of bodily anxiety—castration anxiety in Freudian terms. This is merely a translation of the themes shared in the two productions into technical jargon and a tautology—images that reflect bodily concerns reflect bodily concerns.

We have learned to adopt an *adaptational approach* and insist that valid and dynamic understanding of these images can be developed only if we know the trigger events that Donald's mind was coping with at the time of his daydream and night dreams. We therefore should initiate a *trigger search* using *clues from the themes* of the two creations so we can ascertain the adaptive meanings of these two types of dream images.

Question 4.4

Based on the themes in the manifest contents of these two dreams, suggest some possible trigger events that could have evoked these images.

Answer 4.4

The main themes are those of accident, injury, illness (the dental problem), surgical amputation, self-healing, and flight. The trigger event could therefore be any type of accident or illness, a medical and especially a surgical procedure, a bodily threat of any kind, and possibly some kind of loss or escape.

Let's see what more we learn when we ask Donald to associate to his two dreams.

Donald associates the car accident to a minor fender bender that his son Adam was involved in two days earlier. No one was injured, but it put a scare into Donald, especially since Adam was leaving for college the following weekend. The dentist image brings to mind that Adam had had a wisdom tooth surgically extracted the week before; the procedure had gone well.

Question 4.5

Embedded in the surface contents of these brief associations, which introduce some new themes, is the key trigger for Donald's dreams. What do you think it is?

Answer 4.5

At first, it might seem that Adam's dental surgery and car accident were the main active triggers for these images. However, both of these situations had come to pass and Donald's reactions and coping responses were pretty much spent. Instead, the key trigger event was Adam's pending departure for college. This was a momentous occasion for all concerned and was a trigger that was still active and evoking coping responses in Donald.

Question 4.6

In the spirit of developing a sense of how we process our daydreams, go back to the original pair of dreams and indicate how each of the three trigger events—the accident, the extraction, and Adam's departure—is represented or portrayed in their story lines.

Answer 4.6

The three trigger events, while not mentioned directly, are alluded to—represented—in somewhat different ways in the two dream stories. The car accident and dental procedure both obtained slightly displaced, but easily recognized, portrayals in reference to a car accident and a tooth being pulled. These are thinly disguised allusions or portrayals of the actual trigger events. They could readily come to mind if the incidents were known. They also are in keeping with our earlier speculations which we made without knowing the key triggers.

But the departure of Adam is quite another matter. Even though it is the critical trigger, it is alluded to, or represented through, rather heavily encoded images—walking out of the hospital and floating away from the dentist's office. Each in its own way alludes to a departure. In addition, the loss of a limb and the loss of a tooth also represent Adam's leaving, doing so with even greater disguise than with the escape imagery. These portrayals are truly encoded and would be difficult to suspect, although one could guess that loss might well be an aspect of the trigger situation.

You can see why we need to find the triggers for narrative images and their themes if we are going to make definitive sense of their meanings. You also can see how some triggers can be alluded to directly or with thinly disguised images in our daydreams, while other triggers are heavily encoded and detectable only with added association to the dream images and the pursuit of actual triggering events.

All of these considerations apply equally to daydreams and night dreams. Both are indeed complex communications which share much in common.

In terms of mental mechanisms, we can recognize the operation of both *displacement and disguise or encoding* in creating both dream forms. There are encoded representations of specific incidents by other incidents, and in particular, the representation of Adam's departure by walking away, floating away, and losing a body part. In plain *decoded language,* for Donald, Adam's departure was experienced as an escape from entrapment and bodily harm, however healing it was, and as the loss of a part of his body. This deep, unconscious experience is conveyed in both of Donald dream-type creations.

Notice too that in both dream forms, Donald copes with the sense of physical loss by overcoming the problem—by healing himself in one and by flying away cured in the other. Both dreams have images of successful coping through self-healing and flight.

We see, then, that:

1. Both dreams and daydreams are reactions to emotionally charged trigger events.
2. Both are two-tiered, double-meaning communications; both have direct and encoded meanings.

3. Both show the operation of displacement and disguise in the creation of their surface imagery.
4. Both reflect conscious as well as unconscious efforts at coping.
5 Both contain realistic and unrealistic surface imagery.
6. Night dreams and daydreams seem to be comparable creations of the human imagination—the inventive, coping human mind.

Advantages of Daydreaming

Given the similarities in the structure of night and daydreams, and given their important adaptive messages, we are well-advised to spend time processing both of these narrative creations. I have already developed this process for night dreams[2] and will do the same in this book for our daydreams. However, for the moment, I want to stress that:

- In the name of mental health, you should make it a habit to process your daydreams as often as possible.
- Processing your daydreams will produce comparable results to working with your night dreams.
- There are many advantages to working with daydreams that do not accrue to working with night dreams.

In this light, the following may be said of daydreams:

1. When it comes to human experience and communication, waking daydreams are every bit as compelling and powerful as night dreams.
2. We can learn as much if not more from our waking creations than we can from our sleep dreams.
3. In general, we are able to recall far more daydreams than night dreams, each of them useful in understanding ourselves and our emotional issues. More material generally means more insight.

---

2.   *The Dream Workbook* (Alliance Publishing, 1994).

4. Daydreams have the advantage of being easily recalled simply by noticing you are having or have had one, while most dream images are lost upon awakening and are never retrieved.

5. While some people can be trained to manipulate their dreams through lucid dreaming, everyone can create a daydream on demand and either deliberately orchestrate its story line or allow the mind to go where it will spontaneously. While there may well be many days without a recalled dream, there need be no day without one or more daydream narratives.

6. Daydreams lend themselves well to both surface exploration and trigger decoding efforts.

To paraphrase an oft-quoted comment of Freud regarding sleep dreams, *daydreams rather than night dreams are our most royal road to the "unconscious."*

Exercise 4.1

Let's close this chapter with a few exercises. Take some time for yourself and do the following:

1. Try to remember as many night dreams from the last three days as you can. Then try to remember as many daydreams from the same period. Treat as a daydream any story, short or long, that was on your mind or that you wove into an imaginary scenario. Count the number of each production you have recalled and the number of themes in each collection—and compare the two results.

2. Compare the images and themes of the two sets of stories. Identify similarities and differences.

3. Invent a happy daydream.

4. Create a daydream designed to rework an emotionally charged problem you have been dealing with or expect to confront.

5. Allow your mind the freedom to make up its own daydream, so to speak. Don't plan your topic, but let it emerge spontaneously without censoring or changing the images that come forth.

6. Make up a daydream with notable happenings that are impossible in real life. Allow your imagination full rein—the further out, the better.

7. Finally, if you have any sense of an active trigger or two that concerns you at present, try in some global way to discover the connection between these trigger events and your daydream imagery. If you feel venturesome, associate to the daydream material and see what this adds to your pool of themes and to your understanding. Play with your daydreams; get a feeling for their imagery and range; and try to connect your themes to your triggers to see how much you can learn from bringing them together.

Comment 4.1

The main goals of this exercise are, first, to help you compare night and daydreams, and to see how similar they can be, and second, to get you to pay attention to your daydreams. Daydreams are mental playthings as well as sources of deep and often grave insights. Simply heeding these great creations of your mind will put you on the path to a deeper understanding of their structure and meanings. To promote this effort, let's turn to the many forms that daydream imagery can take.

Daydreams of All Sizes and Shapes

e need two kinds of information to our daydreams:

1. Knowledge of the many forms daydreams can take in addition to those we generate with our own minds and imaginations—a way of maximizing our pool of daydream material and themes.
2. Advice on how to capture and make available as much daydream material as possible.

The more daydream material, the better the results of the processing effort.

Three Ways of Daydreaming

There are three ways we daydream:

1. By creating our own stories within our minds, spontaneously or with deliberate intention. This is *the standard or classical form of daydreaming.*
2. By telling stories to others in a wide range of contexts. This is the *storytelling form of daydreaming—a daydream equivalent.*

3. By borrowing the stories created by others—novelists, news reporters, playwrights, film writers, religious and political leaders, etc. This is the *borrowed form of daydreaming—another daydream equivalent.*

The Standard Form

The standard form of daydreaming is well known. But still there are two points to consider:

1. We tend to think of daydreams as products of our own imaginations that are generated privately during idle or distracted moments. However, we also may shift into the daydreaming mode under a variety of conditions, such as while attending a form of entertainment, talking with others, and the like.

2. We also tend to think of daydreams as extended and elaborate tales. However, every snippet of an imagined event or momentary image constitutes a daydream and can be treated as such.

If you conjure up an image or a story of any kind, you can think of it as your daydream.

Variations on a Creative Form

The central attribute of a daydream is its imagistic or narrative form. This means that any story we tell, to ourselves or others, and any story we've heard or seen that occupies our thoughts, should be thought of as a *daydream equivalent*—a daydream that belongs to us and that needs to be processed.

Storytelling is a universal tendency of the human mind. As a result, there is an overabundance of narrative material generated by ourselves and others, much of it serving, however unwittingly, as daydream forms.

What then are these daydream equivalents? Here is a list of the main ones:

1. *Stories we tell others.*

   a. *Stories that are integrated into a conversation or other type of interaction.* This first form of storytelling is deliberate and an integrated part of a conversation or presentation. The story is used to illustrate or explain something and it is very much a part of what you intend to convey. This type of story is usually dismissed once it has been told, but it has certain properties of daydreams and should be retained and later processed for direct and encoded meanings in light of trigger events—including the circumstances under which the story itself was recounted. The point is to recognize that any story we tell, no matter what the conscious purpose and circumstances, is a daydream equivalent.

      Stories of this kind told to you by others are their daydreams. They become part of your daydreaming activities only when you become preoccupied with their story, thereby recruiting it into your own imagination.

   b. *Marginally related or coincidental stories.* This very common daydream variant involves introducing a story in the course of a conversation that is either entirely unrelated or only peripherally related to the topic at hand.

      For example, two people are talking about business and one suddenly says, "By the way, did you see that newspaper story about the fire, or the murder, or winning the lottery?" Or a married couple is discussing their children and the wife says, "Oh, that reminds me, I meant to tell you about that show I saw on television last night, while you were at the office" and then proceeds to tell her husband what it was about. Or, you are trying to sell computer services to a client. In the course of selling your product, you think of a story about something you think they'd be interested in.

These are all examples of marginally related stories. There's a natural tendency to introduce stories of this kind into all types of conversations—usually without realizing first, that you're telling a story, and second, that it is a daydream equivalent filled with conscious (direct) and unconscious (encoded) meanings. After all, virtually every relationship in which you become involved, no matter how formal or businesslike, has an emotional component that affects the surface interaction and its outcome.

As narratives, these stories are bi-leveled messages filled with direct and encoded meanings. However, the prime trigger event for the marginally related story is easily recognized—it is always in the immediate relationship. That is, we tell someone a marginally related story to communicate our unconscious responses to something the listener has done which is, for us, an emotionally charged trigger event.

Just as it is justifiably said that the person to whom you tell a dream is involved in the dream (in our language, is involved in the evocative trigger event for the dream), the person you tell a coincidental story to has evoked that story from you. He or she therefore is part of the trigger for the story—some aspect of the immediate relationship and interaction with that person has led to the telling of the tale which, in turn, encodes your unconscious perceptions of that person and his or her triggering actions.

Often, simply becoming aware of the story you are telling allows you to identify the trigger to which you are responding. You can then process the story's surface and encoded images to arrive at a measure of insight at that very moment. In addition, you should make note of the narrative so you can later associate to its images and process the material toward further understanding. This is an excellent way to discover your unconscious issues with people with whom you are close or deal with in business and otherwise.

Here too, the marginally related stories told to you by others are their narrative/daydream responses to the triggers you have created for them to process and cope with. Cautious trigger decoding may help you understand their unconscious issues and modify your part in them if need be. And, once again, if you become preoccupied with their narrative, then it becomes one of your own daydreams in need of processing. This is a fascinating moment: a daydream equivalent that has been conjured up in response to a trigger you have created for another person is recruited by you to deal with a trigger event created by someone with whom you have interacted—often enough the very person who told you the story in the first place.

2. *Every story you create, think of, write down, or record in any form is a daydream equivalent.*

3. *Similarly, as noted, every story created by another person that you become preoccupied with or every story you repeat to others also is a daydream equivalent.* The possibilities are endless—a story a relative or friend tells you, a novel you've read, a movie plot, a newspaper or television story, a story in a minister's sermon, etc.

The narratives you choose to think about and work over— any story you become attached to—is a story you have commandeered to serve as one of your own daydreams.

Narrative communications are so crucial to our emotional lives that we've invented countless ways of narrating to ourselves and others.

Exercise 5.1

Spend the next day or two mentally noticing when you shift into the storytelling mode or someone else does so in the course of a conversation—with you or others. Begin to realize just how often narrative imagery occupies your thoughts and musings. Notice too the news and other stories you get attached to and how often you repeat them to others.

Look over the manifest contents of these stories—their surface themes and images, their evident meanings. Realize that these narratives also encode your reaction to emotionally charged trigger events. See if you can discover some of the triggers to which these stories are a coping response. All in all, try to appreciate the potential value of these stories for insight and understanding, and add them to your definition of daydreams.

Comment 5.1

As you have probably discovered, in addition to formal daydreaming, you (and others) spend a great deal of time communicating by means of narrative, daydream equivalent forms. When you begin to listen to yourself and others with the goal of identifying stories in mind, you're likely to be quite amazed at the many variants of daydreams we generate each day and how often they are invoked. Our emotional equilibrium depends on storytelling, much as our survival needs depend on intellectual knowledge to take care of them.

An Illustration

Ned is speaking with Nancy, his co-worker. They are discussing a customer to whom they sell paper goods who complained about the quality of a new product they recently shipped to him. In the course of the conversation, Ned muses that the customer looks like an actor he had seen on television the previous night. He says: "It was the weirdest show. It seems this guy kept coming on to his boss who was this married woman. She put him off until one night, after they closed a deal, she went back to his place. They slept together and, in no time, their whole relationship fell apart and he ended up attempting suicide. What a mess." Ned goes on to say: "We better take back those goods before we lose this guy as a customer."

Question 5.1

What do you make of this marginally related story? What is the likely trigger for the story? What are its main implied or thinly disguised messages? Can you see both a wish and a prohibition here?

Answer 5.1

As you may have guessed, this marginally related story, which *came up consciously* because the customer reminded Ned of an actor he had seen on television, *came up unconsciously* because Ned, who is single, was getting seductive signals from Nancy, who is married.

In general, marginally related stories have little evident surface relevance to the known issues at hand, but are pertinent to the hidden triggers that activate their telling—the emotional side of the immediate relationship. To appreciate the disguised meanings of such a story, were you to tell one, you need to discover its specific trigger. With this type of daydream equivalent, you know where to look first—at the person you are telling the story to and what he or she has done to or with you of late.

Once you have the trigger in hand, you can tap into the surface images for conscious meanings and also trigger decode the encoded messages that the coincidental story contains—all in the service of insight. Later on, you can associate to the story, get a clearer picture of the trigger experience you are working over, and engage in a more careful and thorough assessment of the surface images, and trigger decode their themes to discover their decoded, unconscious meanings.

Ned had been having several spontaneous daydreams about seducing Nancy, but had not acted on his fantasies. That day, Nancy had been subtly seductive. Her overtures had not registered consciously in Ned's mind, but were perceived and processed unconsciously—as evidenced by his coincidental story. With the trigger unconsciously perceived, Ned told his story in all naivete as an unexpected association to their customer. Were that reality absent as a bridge from Ned's unconscious and conscious worlds, you can be certain he would have found another way to express, in displaced and disguised form, the unconscious perceptions and impulses that he was struggling with. Ned's story certainly combines—*condenses*, as we say—his unconscious perceptions of Nancy's seductiveness with his own wishes to seduce her. It also cautions both of them not to act on these conscious and unconscious fantasies and wishes—rightly warning them that their relationship would never be the same and that either or both of them would suffer a suicidal form of guilt. What the conscious mind either blurs or misses entirely, or leads us blindly toward, the deep unconscious mind sees very clearly—which is why we need to capture and process our daydreams as often as possible.

Coincidental Stories as Daydream Equivalents

Note the following regarding coincidental or marginally related stories:

1. Marginally related stories arise as a rule through some superficial, conscious association to the business at hand.
2. There is, however, a hidden *unconscious link* to the present situation as well.
3. A marginally related story always has a bearing on the emotional issues that exist between the storyteller and his or her audience—they are responses to triggers created by the other person or persons present.
4. The principle messages in this type of narrative usually are quite unconscious, although there may be some awareness of aspects of the issues being dealt with in the story. There always is some new knowledge in a disguised story—insights well worth having.
5. The coincidental story is an excellent example of a *displaced and disguised narrative*. The trigger event is related to the present interaction and involves the storyteller and the listener, but the tale that is told is about someone else. The amount of disguise in the story varies, but some encoding is always present.

6. Making use of the marginally related story begins by register-ing the fact that such a story has been told—by you or the other person.

7. While these stories always contain encoded messages, a great deal can be extracted from their surface imagery if you recog-nize the main trigger event that exists between the two parties to the tale—the teller and the listener.

8. As soon as you consider the coincidental story in light of the relationship and triggers at hand, you can explore the surface images in the story as a *valid commentary* on that relationship. This juxtaposition immediately reveals much of the unconscious experience and meaning reflected and encoded in the story.

9. While we consciously deceive ourselves and others a great deal, there is virtually no deception in disguised stories. Deci-pher these stories carefully and use their wisdom to good stead. They are valuable resources there for the taking.

10. Be cautious in reading meaning into the tales told to you by others. There's a lot you don't know about the deeper sources of their marginally related stories, and you do not have their associations to work with. On the one hand, the telling of a coincidental story by someone you are interacting with gener-ally means they are working over unconscious issues related to triggers that you have created for them. It is well to search for these triggers and to process them yourself.

11. With your own stories, you can pick up aspects of their uncon-scious meanings as soon as you tell the tale and link its themes to your triggers. You also can mark the story as a daydream and work with it as part of your nightly reworking of day-dreams from that day. You are then in a good position to come to some sound realizations about the unconscious mean-ings of your coincidental stories—they are a part of your day-dreaming network.

12. Finally, after processing one of your own marginally related sto-ries in light of its immediate triggers, you should search for other trigger events that are also being dealt with by the same tale.

*In all, telling a marginally related story is daydreaming in the
service of immediate adaptive efforts.*

Another Daydream Equivalent

Martha and Victor are married. Martha keeps coming back to a story
she read in the newspaper and saw on television. It was about a married
couple. It seems the wife got pregnant unintentionally and the husband
flipped out, as they put it. He barricaded his wife in their bedroom and
refused to let her out. He pulled the telephone outlet from the wall and
the house was so isolated that her cries for help could not be heard. The
situation was resolved only because the husband had inadvertently left
his carrying case in the bedroom and the wife discovered his portable
telephone inside the case. She called the police and they freed her; the
man was hospitalized in a psychiatric institution.

Question 5.2

*Here is a story someone is repeating in her mind, a story told to
her husband several times. Try to guess what the trigger event is for
this story. What issue does Martha seem to be working over? Who is
the problem connected with? Use the themes of the story as clues to
your answers.*

Answer 5.2

When the human mind is at a loss to create its own daydreams,
there are countless stories that others have created for us to use. The
world is filled with narrative communications and we are motivated
by strong unseen needs to express our unconscious concerns and
visions. As needed, we borrow suitable creations wrought by others
or created by real events and adopt them as our daydreams, aptly
fashioned to deliver our own unconscious messages.

To answer the question, the trigger event here is an ongoing dispute between Martha and Victor. Martha has been unable to get pregnant and wants to adopt a child, while Victor doesn't want to. They have discussed their conflict from time to time, but neither has given any ground. Martha feels Victor's objections are unfounded, while Victor doesn't exactly know why—perhaps it's the inconvenience of having to care for a child—but he's dead set against adoption.

They had not discussed the problem for some time, but it came up again the day before Martha had become preoccupied with this news story—with much the same stalemated outcome. She had borrowed this story to deal with two interrelated, reactivated triggers: first, Victor's failure to impregnate her, and second, Victor's opposition to adoption. It is important to realize that Victor's actions and attitudes are Martha's triggers (just as Martha's behaviors are Victor's triggers—adaptation always begins with outside stimuli and events).

In light of the trigger events, we can see that the themes of the story deal mainly with getting pregnant and touch on having a child. The news story is a thinly disguised, displaced, and encoded representation of Martha's triggers. These shared themes *bridge* from the narrative story to the trigger event, indicating that the two are related.

We therefore can turn now to the images and themes to see what Martha is communicating unconsciously about her two evocative triggers. Her main borrowed message is that the man, the stand in for or representation of Victor, is insanely opposed to his wife's having a child. The theme of entrapment is also prominent. Put together, they indicate that Martha's unconscious perception and appraisal of her husband is that he is terrified of bringing a baby into their marriage for fear he won't be able to handle the intrusion and responsibility, and that he will be entrapped and go insane.

There's a great deal of truth to these disguised impressions. They explain why Martha has been unable to change Victor's mind about adopting a child. Without his realizing it consciously, he is terrified to do so. Most conscious disagreements are fueled by unconscious fears of this kind, which is why these direct disputes seldom get resolved. But once you tap into the unconscious issues motivating your position and that of the other person, it becomes possible to rework and resolve their very powerful, previously concealed aspects.

Much of our conscious behavior and choices is powerfully fueled by unconscious perceptions and needs. It is by deciphering the disguised messages in our daydreams that we can access these unconscious forces and resolve their detrimental effects. This particular moment was the beginning of such efforts by Martha and Victor.

Borrowed daydreams show us we are all part of a family of daydreamers.

With this realization, let's turn to the next chapter and the strategies available for capturing and retaining our daydream images.

Capturing Your Daydreams

Having established the range of daydream forms, we turn now to the means by which we can ensure that we consciously realize we've had a daydream and preserve its contents. Obviously, this is the first step in processing our daydreams and the more efficient we become, the greater the opportunity for deep and compelling insights.

The Nonrecording of Daydreams

When it comes to remembering daydream images, many people immediately think of picking up a pen or pencil to write down their images. Their justification is founded in the advice given by many dreams researchers—that we should record our dreams as soon as we awake. This advice overlooks some decisive factors that speak against such practices.

There is, then, a critical constraint that is vital to the sound and effective processing of daydream material. In essence it is this:

Daydreams are products of human nature and need to be allowed to unfold as part of spontaneous human experience. This means daydreams should never be written down or recorded in any way, because to do so takes them out of your mind and into the external world. As recorded events, written daydreams are treated very differently from those that are simply kept in one's mind, where they are a living part of who you are and how you cope with emotionally charged concerns and trigger events. In substance, then, to allow daydreams to live and breathe, to reveal their essences, and to help you as much as any human invention is able to do, not a single word should ever be recorded in any fashion.

Many people object to this constraint. They rationalize that they will forget their daydreams if they do not write them down. But we already know that if that happens, all you need to do is make up a fresh daydream story and you'll have plenty of material to process.

There is no valid exception to this principle. Objections to non-recording is largely based on the universal fear of encoded narrative messages and their unconscious perceptions and meanings—meanings that are destroyed when a daydream is put on paper.

Recording a daydream would be something like taking the engine out of a car to examine it. You can look at the engine and see a lot of things, but you can never comprehend its role in the total system that makes up the operating car. Similarly, you can isolate a daydream and treat it as a fixed specimen, but you lose all chance to understand the place of that daydream in the dynamic flow and adaptations of your life.

Along different lines, it is important to know when you're remembering many daydreams, as opposed to only a few or none. When recall is at its height, you probably have some strong emotional issues you're trying to deal with. When recall is sparse, it can imply either that you're at relative peace with yourself and the world or that you're dealing with some extremely difficult trigger situations.

In the latter instance, the sparseness of daydream material has probably come about because you're somewhat overwhelmed by highly traumatic triggers. Fearful of the impact that these trigger events are having on you unconsciously, you try to shut off your deep unconscious mind by failing to recall your daydream images so you can avoid processing them toward deep insight. But this situation actually should motivate you to invent a couple of daydreams and subject them to processing—in the emotional realm, excessive defensiveness, obliteration, and ignorance are costly defenses.

In principle, the fewer daydreams you recall on a given day, the greater the need to create fresh daydream imagery for processing. This rule applies because the more severe the trigger, the greater the wish of the conscious system to divorce itself from the unconscious experience of the trigger event. Creating your own daydreams counteracts the effects of this natural, but costly, defensiveness.

The Requisites for Processing

Let's elaborate now on what is needed to process your daydreams. Before you can rework, use, and benefit from these inventions, you have to:

1. Know that you've had a daydream.
2. Remember as much as possible about its contents.
3. Be able to deliberately create one or more daydreams as needed.
4. Set aside time to work with and process your pool of daydream material.
5. Learn how to process a daydream for meaning and adaptive solutions, as reflected directly on its surface and camouflaged in that same surface imagery.

You've got to catch a genie before you can benefit from her magical powers; so too, you've got to catch a daydream before you can benefit from its potential wisdom.

Two Types of Personal Daydreams

There are two types of personal daydreams:

1. Those that unfold without deliberate effort, as part of your inevitable daydreaming activities.

2. Those that are composed with full intention of doing so.

1. *Spontaneous daydreams.* We spend about half of our waking hours daydreaming. All too often, we don't realize we've had a daydream and the resource is lost.

The first step in processing and benefitting from a spontaneous daydream is to pause, so you register consciously that you've had the daydream and fix its contents in your mind. In the course of any given day, you are likely to have many different unplanned daydreams. The human mind is designed to daydream; it has a natural, inbuilt propensity for moving in and out of narrative communications and daydreaming is a major expression of this tendency. Though you may lose much of your daydream imagery, heeding these lapses into fantasy, short or long, will provide an abundance of daydream material for later processing.

Create a mind-set so you're ready to catch your spontaneous daydreams before they fade into oblivion.

Exercise 6.1

Try to remember the last spontaneous daydream you had, and a couple daydreams prior to that. See how many you can recall from the past 24 hours. Keep practicing and see if your daydream memory improves—as it should.

Comment 6.1

How well did you do? Chances are you initially lost most of your daydream material. I have already suggested that the main reason for this loss lies with human dread of unconscious perceptions encoded into these creations. We therefore must make a deliberate effort to fix our spontaneous daydreams in our minds and see that we process them at some point so we can uncover the invaluable information and meaning they contain.

A closer look at the situation, however, indicates that while the conscious mind is inclined to forget daydreams, it also has a built-in need to express its encoded unconscious messages through these same inventions. This results in something akin to what evolutionists call an arms race: the need to communicate pitted against the need to obliterate. It turns out the human mind has evolved in ways that favor defensive obliteration over memory, and ignorance over knowledge—ergo, the forgetting of most daydreams.

Still, the battle is not lost. Evolution also has provided us with a critical faculty essentially lacking in all other animals—the ability to consciously override our natural givens and inclinations. Thus, we, as humans, have the capability, should we choose to exercise it, to overcome our defensive needs and remember our daydreams rather than letting them slip away. We can learn to mark our daydreams, catch them as soon as we've had them, and process them immediately if time permits, or store them for future processing—for example, before going to sleep at night.

In invoking this determination to remember your daydreams, you will probably be surprised at how difficult it is to keep this resolve. You should be prepared to experience the defensive tendency of your mind to let its narratives slip away and their encoded messages with them. Because both are encoded stories, daydreams and night dreams tend to elude much of the recall process. With daydreams, however, we're awake and can be alert to catching them when they materialize; beyond that, we can defy nature by simply composing a daydream on the spot.

2. *The deliberately created daydream.*

As I have emphasized, all is not lost if you forget your spontaneous daydreams. All you need to do is set aside some time to create one or more daydreams and they will, with effort, most certainly come to mind.

There are two types of engineered daydreams:

  a. Those that are created by design, with specific contents in mind.

  b. Those you generate simply by deciding to create a daydream without any pre-formed plan, and letting the inclinations of your mind do the rest.

In general, daydreams that are made-to-order are of the *escapist*, creative denial, and positive kind, while those that are allowed to resemble spontaneous daydreams tend to be of the *meaning only* type—and especially loaded with conscious and unconscious meanings.

Daydreams are best created during moments that do not require much conscious attention and effort. The activities that permit daydreaming include: lying in bed after waking or before falling asleep; driving a car or riding public transportation; rest periods at work or in general; and other moments spent alone during the day or night. It is wise to choose a time when you can have as many daydreams as you wish, and can, if you are so inclined, process them on the spot, to uncover their deeper meanings.

Catching Your Daydreams

Let's think about things you can do to facilitate the capture of your spontaneous daydreams.

Question 6.1

What can you do to increase the number of daydreams you become aware of consciously and retain?

Answer 6.1

The following is a list of aids for remembering your daydreams (and, of course, writing them down is not one of them; see above):

1. Maintain a daydream alert—be daydream sensitive.
2. Build into your thinking the realization that you actually have many daydreams, some very brief, others quite lengthy.
3. While you want to allow your daydreams to flow easily and unfold spontaneously, it is helpful to have a background sense that you're in the midst of daydreaming as the images unfold.

This enables you to be fully aware of the daydream as soon as you're finished.

4. Learn how to work with and benefit from your daydreams. Your appreciation of their value will motivate you and enable you to better remember your daydreams.

Hopefully, you are now in a position to capture a large number of daydreams for processing for your personal benefit. Let's carry out two final exercises to close this chapter.

Exercise 6.2

Over the next three days, work on remembering your daydreams. Make use of the methods suggested above. At the end of each day, while lying in bed before going to sleep, list in your mind every daydream you can recall. Get a sense of how many you've had and how elaborate they are. Notice too the kinds of themes they reflect, the amount of power they possess, and any other conspicuous features.

Compare the harvest of daydreams from each of these three nights. Notice repetitive themes, variations in the amount of recall, and the like. If you have time, try to determine the main trigger events that concerned you on each of these days. Is there a correlation between the severity of your main trigger events and the amount of material you remembered? That is, did the most severe triggers prompt you to recall the most or the least amount of daydream imagery?

Comment 6.2

The main purpose of this exercise is to further introduce you to your daydreams and their themes, to promote your interest in these products of your imagination, and to enhance your ability to recall their imagery. In general, the more severe the traumatic trigger event, the greater the number of daydreams you will recall. However, as you may discover, if the trauma is extreme, paradoxically, you may find recall extremely difficult. At times of major insults to the psyche, the human mind goes into a highly defensive and obliterating mode of expression, even on the deep, unconscious level. You are well-advised to give yourself plenty of time before pressing for the encoded meanings and unconscious experience of these overly intense trigger events (see chapters 7 and 8).

Exercise 6.3

As a final exercise for this chapter, on each of the next three nights, take the time to create one or more deliberately invented daydreams. Push the story through to an ending, and conjure up additional stories if you are so inclined. Then compare the themes of your spontaneous and purposely imagined daydreams. Are they similar or different, and in what ways? Does one set seem more positive than the other set, more hopeful or hopeless? Notice as much as you can about each group of daydreams.

Comment 6.3

There are no hard and fast rules about the themes of these two types of daydreams. However, it is not uncommon to find that spontaneous daydreams tend to be more grim than those we deliberately create. Certainly, you have far more control over the second kind of daydream, and if desired, you can give them a far more positive cast than otherwise. On the other hand, if you are tailoring a daydream to an emotional issue, it may well include images with power and pain.

With this, we complete our overview of the world of daydreaming and daydreams. It's time to study how we can put daydream power to use for ourselves every day of our lives. We'll begin with creative denial and proceed from there.

PART II

Daydreams in Action

CHAPTER 7

Daydreams and Creative Denial

As we have seen, at bottom daydreams are distinctive mental coping responses to emotionally charged trigger events or issues. However, we also know that daydreams can be shaped in two ways:

1. To reinforce denial and drive positive images—*the escapist–denial daydream* which encodes meaning as well.
2. To generate direct and encoded meaning for processing towards insight—*the meaning only or insight-producing daydream.*

We must now consider a critical principle:

The type of daydream we invoke and what we choose to do with its imagery depends to a significant extent on the nature of the trigger event with which we are coping.

To clarify this point, let's develop a classification of trigger events—stresses and traumas—to see how they relate to the way in which we use our daydream images. Broadly speaking, there are two classes of trigger events:

1. *Mild to moderate* stresses, traumas, and conflict-laden emotionally tinged choices.
2. *Severe to overwhelming* stresses, traumas, and conflict-laden choices.

Mild to Moderately Stressful Trigger Events

We would place most of life's exigencies, common everyday issues and emotional conflicts, in the first group. This group includes illnesses and injuries that are not life-threatening; most job-related and personal life choices, such as career decisions, friendship, and marital preferences, affiliations of all kinds, and a wide range of similar events or decisions; all manner of stresses and traumas to yourself and your loved ones that fall short of jeopardizing anyone's existence—job loss, divorce, children leaving home, translocation, rejections of all kinds, etc; and an enormously wide range of other kinds of frustrations, conflicts, hurts, and even moments of success.

Each day, then, our lives are filled with mild to moderate stresses and strains, trigger events whose meanings are perceived both consciously and unconsciously and then reworked and processed toward an adaptive response. The unconscious reactions are critical determinants of how we respond not only to the trigger experience itself, but, through the ever-present use of displacement, to other situations and individuals.

The effects of emotionally charged triggers, as mediated through both conscious and unconscious processes, are far-reaching.

Meaning is critical to the experience and consequences of triggers and to their processing. Mild to moderate triggers are deeply meaningful and call for trigger decoding our responsive daydream images. Failure to do so leaves us at the mercy of our unrecognized *unconscious* conflicts and needs. We then lead much of our emotional lives defensively through *displacement* and suffer the inevitable consequences of misplaced reactions and failed adaptations.

In processing the many mild to moderate trigger events we need to adapt to each day, it is essential to:

1. Select for processing the most significant stressors with which you are currently trying to cope.

2. Process your daydreams toward an appreciation of your conscious and especially unconscious experience of the issues involved, seeking the best possible adaptive responses to these issues based on both superficial and deep understanding.

The essential point, then, is that with minor and moderate trigger events you should process your daydreams toward insight and adaptive solutions.

With this much understood, I will postpone our investigation of how we use our daydreams to gain insight. We must first take a careful look at how we use our daydreams in response to more major and overwhelming traumatic situations.

Severely Stressful Trigger Events

How do we best utilize our daydreams in the face of major stresses and traumas?

This class of trigger events is essentially defined by the presence of a threat to the life of the daydreamer or someone close to him or her, or by the actual death of a loved one. Included here are serious accidents, injuries, illnesses, loss through death, and the like.

Our use of daydreams under these circumstances must be carried forth in light of an understanding of how the human mind is programmed to deal with traumas of this kind—essentially, how we deal with death and the death anxieties these events mobilize.

Let's begin this exploration with a question.

Exercise 7.1

Recall the most recent major trauma you have experienced. Then recall the most severe trauma you've experienced in your life. Answer the following questions for both of these traumas.

Who was involved in the event? What was your part in it? Can you remember any daydreams (or night dreams) from that period of your life? If you can, were they related to the incident in any way, or were they far removed from it? How else did you handle the trauma? In principle, how do you think we mainly deal with actual or threatened severe hurts and losses of this kind?

Comment 7.1

There is a common pattern in our response to a death, especially if it involves an accident or sudden loss, or a threat to our own life. The tendency is to shut down our processing systems because of the terror and helplessness the meanings of these triggers hold. We fail to remember night dreams at all, while the daydreams we do recall or create are mainly a reworking of the trauma—often with denial generating a different, nonfatal outcome. With time, night dreams of the event itself begin to appear, while daydreams continue to rework the *conscious* experience of the trigger event and other possible outcomes. Efforts to process these daydreams for deeper, encoded meanings that reveal the *deep unconscious experience* of the trigger event tend to be shallow and to add little that has not been experienced consciously and that is not already known.

In the face of possible or pending personal death, there is little movement toward accessing unconscious meanings, but positive, optimistic, illness-healing and illness-denying daydreams (and sometimes night dreams as well) often begin to materialize. The situation often remains this way until the end.

On the other hand, if a personal threat of death passes or another person dies, the denial type of daydream eventually gives way to other kinds of imagery. In time it becomes possible to extract unconscious meaning by processing your daydreams toward both conscious and unconscious insights, including those that come from trigger decoding.

In essence, then, when death looms large, the human mind and its daydreaming function are geared toward *denial,* in lieu of meaning.

Once the loss has been experienced or the threat of death passes, the mind and its daydreams become open to *meaning* even though denial remains. This translates into the following precepts:

1. Upon the threat of death or during a severe loss, we are best advised to use daydreams to support our denial/escapist efforts and to try to ensure that they involve *creative rather than dysfunctional forms of denial.*
2. When the threat of death becomes more removed, we should process our daydreams toward direct and trigger decoded insights.
3. Generate escapist daydreams when death is at hand, and non-escapist, meaning daydreams when the threat of death has diminished.

Creative Denial

The emotion-processing mind has evolved with two fundamental psychological defenses:

1. *Denial*—a mental mechanism and defense through which an individual obliterates the existence or presence of a self-evident, usually traumatic, reality.
2. *Repression*—a mental mechanism through which we fail to remember potentially upsetting memories and incidents.

Both defenses are motivated by anxiety, pain, and disturbing meanings and experiences. They are dynamically activated out of human need rather than simple, mechanical errors of observation or recall. Both serve adaptation, but they may do so in successful fashion without undue cost and consequent pain (normal or creative denial and repression) or be overly costly (dysfunctional or maladaptive uses of these two mechanisms).

Unfortunately, the denial defense has acquired a bad reputation and is often thought of as inherently sick, inappropriate, and even psychotic. While there are indeed dysfunctional uses of denial, *this mental defense is a basic means through which we get through each day.* I refer here to the inevitable and creative and healthy use of the denial of personal death without which we'd barely survive. Indeed, it is quite likely that defensive denial first appeared in humans when they first became aware of personal death, some 150,000 years ago.

There are many forms of denial. As a perspective for the denial functions of daydreaming and daydreams, I will list the main ones here:

1. *Psychotic denial* is seen when denial interferes with a person's contact with reality. The classic example is the woman holding a pillow in her arms, believing that it is her dead child and thereby denying the child's death. Most forms of denial do not entail a break with reality because they involve isolated issues that do not otherwise interfere with how we function.

2. *Denial through action* is seen when a person does something designed to obliterate or distract him or her from the awareness of a painful reality. Illicit affairs after a major loss or illness often are unconsciously designed to deny that loss. Most impulsive, blind, and irrational actions that have not been sufficiently thought through are used to distract an individual from and to deny some painful event.

   A more socially accepted form of denial through action is seen with Mardi Gras and other celebrations where usually forbidden behaviors are allowed expression and their negative consequences are obliterated. These moments are used to deny both painful realities and underlying feelings of depression, whatever their cause.

3. *Denial in thought and fantasy* is a means by which painful realities simply are set aside, usually by generating images of happy, positive, celebratory, manicy, marvelous, and miraculous happenings. There is a fine line between healthy and unhealthy, creative and maladaptive forms of this kind of denial. On one side, the denial and escape often is a great relief to the fantasizer, and may well promote healing and emotional stability. On the other side, there is the danger that the use of denial in thought and fantasy will be so intense that it will interfere with taking adaptive action regarding the denied problem or otherwise interfere with the functioning of the denier.

4. *Denial of illness* is universal, and while it may bring temporary relief, its extended use will preclude the pursuit of necessary medical care and can be fatal. Similarly, denial of death also is a universal defense, but when it is overused, there are detrimental consequences. For example, denying the death of a loved one will interfere with the healthy mourning process and usually lead to blind actions designed at great emotional cost to support the mental use of denial. Denial of death also can lead to dangerous, reckless behaviors because the denial impairs a person's assessment of danger and other aspects of reality.

Using denial creatively and with minimal cost is an essential mental defense, but it must be used with caution because overuse can be dangerous to your mental and physical health.

Daydreams and Creative Denial

Daydreams are a primary vehicle for images in the service of creative denial. The generation of denial or escapist daydreams can be quite adaptive and can aid one in coping with psychologically overwhelming situations. Some common types of creative denial daydreams are:

1. *Denial by revising reality*, through which we review a seriously traumatic situation and change the outcome for the better. In this form of denial, the actual reality is acknowledged and then changed. A simple example involves a fatal car accident after which the driver goes over and over again in his or her imagination the things he or she could have done differently so there would have been no fatality.

2. *Denial by avoidance*, in which daydreams are created that do not in any way allude to or touch on the painful trauma at hand. This type of denial usually is buttressed by other avoidance mechanisms.

3. *Denial through positive imagery*, in which highly positive daydreams predominate. This is seen in people who are ill and

daydream of magical cures, of being well, of paradise islands, happy moments, and the like. The positive images shut out and replace the grim situation with which the individual is faced.

Up to a point, denial in fantasy is a healthy and adaptive form of daydreaming, but there always is the danger of a shift to action forms of denial that carry great risks of harm to self and others.

Major Traumas and Creative Denial

The human mind has evolved a single fundamental way of dealing with major traumas and the death anxiety that they engender—the use of denial in its myriad of forms, including escapist daydreams. There is some evidence that in its most creative forms, this kind of denial can be psychologically and physically self-protective, and that, supported by proper medical care, it can reverse the course of some physical illnesses.

The following can be said about how humans respond to and cope with death-related traumas:

1. As is true of all systems in the universe, including biological systems, the emotion-processing mind has a limited capacity to deal with stress and trauma—beyond which there is dysfunction or collapse. Major traumas overwhelm the coping capacities of the human mind. They evoke feelings of panic, anxiety, and depression, and the processing of information and meaning is severely impaired.

2. When death anxiety is intense, the conscious system becomes impaired and direct insights are very difficult or impossible to develop. The deep unconscious system usually shuts down entirely and there are few if any decodable stories available for processing. Highly defensive, obliterating mechanisms take over and denial reigns supreme.

3. When death is involved, there are few satisfying adaptive answers. The best strategy is to cope without harming yourself

and/or others and to make use of denial within safe limits and with inventiveness.

4. Creative denial through the invocation of intensely positive daydreams is an important aspect of how we cope with activated death anxiety—do not demur from using it.

5. The use of denial should not preclude proper medical care.

6. As time passes and death looms less large, the mind recovers its processing capacities and some degree of insight becomes possible on both the conscious and unconscious levels of understanding. Encoded daydreams appear and it becomes possible to process and decode their storylines toward meaning.

In the face of a major trauma, be prepared to shift from creative denial to the pursuit of insight as the threat of death either passes or an actual death begins to fade into the past.

7. There are several common ways we respond to severe trauma:

   a. By developing seeming insights that actually are forms of denial—false insights designed consciously or unconsciously to undo the threat or experience of severe loss or harm. Finding a way of believing that a fatal illness will not be fatal is an example of this kind of self-deceptive denial couched as a way of understanding.

   b. By adopting personal or shared beliefs that cannot be proven or disproven in reality, usually the kind that deny death and loss. Examples of this form of denial are beliefs in past lives, channelling, contacts with deceased people, belief in God and life after death, and so on. For those who adopt such beliefs, they generally become unassailable ways of denying the finality of death.

   c. Developing realistic and unrealistic perspectives about the meaning of life and death. Everyone has, in some form, however explicit or poorly articulated, a philosophy about death. Some see death as part of life, some accept its inevitability with seeming tranquility, some see it as a terrible ending that must be endured, and so forth. In general, these positions serve to lessen death anxiety through either some form of denial or by facing reality in a way that facilitates adaptation.

d. Generating conscious and especially unconscious insights into the specific meanings of a given threat of death or actual loss for the daydreamer—whether it's facing one's own demise or that of an important other. Being able to develop these insights is vital to coming to terms with a significant loss and for long-term recovery from the effects of these traumas.

We need to realize that denial brings immediate relief, but it also interferes with the development of insight and sound coping skills. Trigger decoding and insight, however, bring relief and perspectives that enhance present and future adaptations.

In essence, then, denial precludes learning.

Daydreaming plays an important role in our responses to activated death anxiety. In these situations, you are well-served by remembering your daydream stories and spending time creating daydreams and processing the entire output.

In reacting to severe traumas, daydreams rather than night dreams offer the best opportunity for flexible responses as varied as blatant denial and deep insight.

With this in mind, let's turn in the next chapter to two illustrations of these issues and their daydream-based solutions.

CHAPTER 8

Major Trauma and Escapist Solutions

Let's turn to two vignettes to further develop the escapist uses of daydreams presented in the previous chapter.

Suffering a Loss: An Illustration

Dan and Edna are siblings; both are in their early 40s. Their oldest brother Frank died suddenly of a massive heart attack. Both siblings suffered the grief and pain of sudden loss, and shared the mourning period by reminiscing, wondering about the frailty of life, generating wishful fantasies that he was still alive, and more.

This kind of conscious mourning work, which usually includes denial-based fantasies, is an essential part of coping with personal loss. But often, we need something more to prevent dysfunction, and daydreams can and should play a notable role in these added efforts. Let's see how Dan turned to daydreaming for this help and how it worked for him.

Dan's conscious problem with Frank was that he didn't like or trust his brother. Dan was convinced that when their father died, Frank had appropriated some of the assets in their father's estate for himself, without telling the rest of the family. Dan was unable to confirm his suspicions, but a tension developed between the two that never got resolved.

Dan wished he somehow could have made peace with his brother before he died. The loss left him with a feeling of unfinished business and a persistent sense of guilt for suspecting his brother of wrongdoing. Dan's conscious efforts to tell himself he was wrong to feel as he did had little or no effect. He tried working over his conflict and guilt with Edna and others, but nothing got resolved. He realized this was a time to turn to his daydreams for help, and that is what he did.

In principle, we should turn to our daydreams at times of unresolved stress and conflict. Properly processed, they can point us toward invaluable and otherwise undiscovered answers to life's problems.

Dan sat down in a comfortable chair in his den one evening, soon after his brother had died; he was alone. He decided to pursue his daydreams, to ask them for help, so to speak. He relived his busy day at work and thought about his more idle moments to see if he could recover any of his spontaneous daydreams. But even though he had tried to mark them for later processing, he lost most of what he had conjured up.

With some effort, he did recall imagining that his brother was still alive. Dan saw himself telephoning his brother and suggesting that they meet for coffee; Frank obliges. In the course of their imaginary conversation, Dan brings up the doubts he has about his brother's honesty with their father's estate. Frank is able to explain the seemingly suspicious behaviors on which Dan had built his mistrust, and Dan apologizes for having been so suspicious. The two brothers embrace and part as friends and buddies once again.

Question 8.1

What type of daydream is this? Do you think it will be sufficient to help Dan resolve his still simmering conflicts with Frank?

Answer 8.1

This is indeed an *escapist/creative denial* daydream. Dan felt better for having had and thinking over this daydream. Would that it were so, he muttered to himself. But the daydream image soon gave way to a renewal of his mistrust of Frank—nothing had been settled. The denial daydream quickly lost its power and the anger Dan felt toward Frank and his reactive guilt returned full force. It was a nice moment, but nothing had really changed.

> *When escapist/denial daydreams don't work, press on, generate a fresh set of daydreams, and search for some kind of insight with which to resolve the underlying unconscious issues that are fueling the conflict and guilt.*

Unable to recall any other spontaneous daydreams from his day, Dan sat back and allowed his mind to wander in search of a fresh imaginary story. In time, he began to weave a tale. It was based on an incident that had occurred some ten years earlier. At first, he went over the event itself, imagining himself going to his father to borrow $10,000. What had actually happened, Dan reminded himself, was that his father had gotten quite angry with Dan, who needed the money to pay off a personal loan he'd not been able to cover with his income. His father had finally but begrudgingly lent Dan the money, and threatened to cut Dan off from his inheritance if he didn't pay back the loan in due time.

In his daydream, however, Dan imagines a friendly discussion with his father and a great deal of compassion and understanding on his father's part. His father is glad to lend him the money, and Dan promises to pay his father back.

Time passes in Dan's daydream and he next creates a scene in which he and his father are having dinner together at his father's club; Dan's father tells him he needn't pay back the loan—he should keep the money as a gift. More time passes, and Dan pictures himself having some extra money and telling his two siblings about the loan and giving them each a third of the amount he had borrowed.

Dan stopped daydreaming at this juncture and looked over his images. The thought of the loan had crossed his mind once or twice while mourning the loss of his brother, but each time he had allowed it to quickly pass into oblivion. The fact was Dan had not yet paid back the loan, nor had he told either sibling about it. Yet, he was putting the loan at the center of his daydream. Why so?

Question 8.2

In thinking about Dan's daydream in light of its trigger—the death of his brother Frank—what insight can you get from its images and themes? What coping response does the story suggest to Dan— that is, according to the daydream, what can he do to make greater peace with his loss?

Answer 8.2

The healthy mourning process involves a slow rework and resolution of the specific issues and unresolved conflicts the mourner had with the person who died. Nothing in human adaptation is global and general, everything is specific. Thus, you cannot simply say you must come to terms with the death of so-and-so. Instead, you must find ways—and daydreams are among them—to discover your specific unresolved problems with the deceased and work them out in some genuine way that gives you a measure of peace. If not, the unconscious meanings of the loss and the unresolved conflicts with the deceased will haunt you for an indefinite period and may adversely affect your behavior without your realizing it.

In Dan's case, his daydream reveals that one significant source of his unresolved guilt vis-à-vis Frank is the secret loan that he had obtained from his father and never paid back. Consciously, Dan traced his guilt to being overly suspicious of his brother and to never having made peace with him. But his daydream indicates there's another unresolved issue between Dan and his brother, another source of his guilt—Dan's secret loan.

Spontaneous daydreams and the creation of free-flowing daydream images are remarkable markers of our unconscious conflicts and issues. What our overly defensive conscious minds cannot ascertain directly is often revealed when we release the mind to its own wanderings.

It is typical of the emotion-processing mind to focus on obvious problems that are real but relatively inconsequential, to cover more serious, repressed problems that unconsciously derail our feelings and functioning. In Dan's case, the guilt over suspecting his brother of cheating covered the more serious guilt Dan had over his own duplicity—which he had been attributing to or projecting onto Frank and then reacting adversely to his own projection of himself.

Dan knew fully well that each of his siblings deserved one-third of the money he had received from his father. The daydream not only pointed to a hidden source of guilt, it also offered Dan a solution to that guilt—an effective coping response. The story indicated that if Dan wanted to make peace with his brother—and his sister—he should tell his brother's wife and sister about the loan and pay them their due when he could. In this way, he could resolve a portion of his conflict with his brother and better accept his loss. Such are the gains offered by the surface images of a daydream when they are placed into the proper context or trigger situation.

Returning to Dan, once he finished processing his daydream, he remembered that he had made a very bad business decision that week and it had cost him some $3,000—a sum very close to what he owed each sibling. With some further work, he was able to trace his blunder to his *unconscious guilt* and need for punishment and suffering because he had cheated his siblings. An error he had dismissed as poor business judgment actually had been fueled by a major unrecognized, unconscious source—his own dishonesty with his siblings.

Without realizing it, a large part of our daily lives is governed by unconscious forces that can be brought to light mainly by processing our daydreams.

Some Useful Principles

Let's conclude this part of our discussion by stating these principles:

1. Whenever you suffer a major loss or the death of someone close to you—or any major trauma—turn to your daydreams for assistance in working through the unresolved emotional issues raised by the experience. Become accustomed to thinking of daydreams as a major adaptive resource.

2. Anticipate the emergence of denial-based, escapist daydreams immediately after the trauma. They will emerge spontaneously and can be created deliberately as well. Accept the reassurance offer and if they bring you some peace, so much the better.

3. With the loss of others, however, denial is of limited help in that the death cannot be denied without causing disruptions in how you act and function. The unconscious issues the loss has created will continue to fester outside of awareness until you use your daydreams to discover what the issues are and how to resolve them.

4. In dealing with the death of others, denial should be supplemented with a search for and the achievement of insight by processing your daydream images.

5. When concerned with or anticipating the death of a loved one, denial is also of service, but here too adding a measure of insight is extremely helpful. Denying a fatal illness in a loved one may lessen the pain, but it also eliminates the possibility of making peace with that person and with yourself as death approaches. Escapist daydreams should be supplemented by insight-producing stories.

6. Similar principles apply to all major traumas.

A creative combination of denial and insight will serve you best.

Facing Serious Personal Illness

The situation is both similar and different to experiencing the death of another person when facing a serious or life-threatening illness yourself. In these instances, there is a powerful battle waged between denying that death is imminent and dealing with the anxieties and real issues raised by the expectation of dying.

For most people, creative denial does most of the work and is either sustained throughout the experience or surrendered for brief moments when the escapism fails to sustain their emotional equilibrium. Here too, both escapist and insight-producing daydreams can play a role in coping with the situation. It is well to stress again that there are indeed *healthy and creative forms of denial.*

Whatever your personal belief system, it must deal with the evident finality of death, which is the end of life. While you may choose consciously to embrace one of the many hopefully creative denial systems that undo the finality of death, a part of your mind will still need assistance in coping with the fearful aspects of this inevitability. Fantasies of life after death, in any form, are daydream formations, and being able to successfully invest in this kind of daydream may help a person endure a confrontation with a serious illness and the promise of a life about to end.

Denial-based Daydreams

Denial of death has many forms and shapes, among them the many different kinds of *denial-based daydreams.* These fantasy formations can be classified as follows:

1. *Formal life-after-death systems, group denial of death.* Examples include beliefs in past and future lives, religious beliefs in an everlasting soul, contacts with the dead through mediums, and the like. There are narrative elements to all of these belief systems which usually extend into personal daydreams, especially at times of great threat. These systems vary from total denial of death to the belief in an afterlife that acknowledges death, but views it without any sense of finality.

2. *Personal beliefs or myths.* These are individual daydream formations that do not fit into the usual forms of group denial systems. Many people create their own scenarios regarding

some form of afterlife, and they often rehearse and retell the stories that support their beliefs. Here too, the extent of denial may vary from an outright denial of personal death to acceptance of death with a view of life eternal.

3. *Denial of illness.* In addition to these global fantasy formations, as noted in the previous chapter, ill-fated individuals often respond to diagnoses of fatal illnesses with a degree of denial that involves outright denial of the illness, a strong belief in misdiagnosis, and/or the denial of its life-threatening qualities.

It is rare if not impossible for a person to face death without moments of denial.

4. *The deliberate creation of positive daydreams.* These daydreams are a means of denying pending death through stories of well-being, healing, miraculous cure, and other kinds of happy events completely divorced from the existing crisis. This forced positive imagery is usually thought of as generating cheerful images as a form of support and succor, while the denial aspect of the imagery is overlooked largely because of the unfortunate negative connotations of the term *denial* even when the mechanism is used for healing. However, these often wondrous daydreams do serve to deny threat and can be used with considerable creativity for the relief they may bring.

Some Words of Caution

There are some caveats in invoking these escapist/denial daydreams. Because most people fervently seek to obliterate all semblance of death anxiety, the following points seem prudent:

1. It is inadvisable for outsiders to tamper with a dying person's use of denial unless the usage notably interferes with the dying person's life or harms others.

2. In the face of a threat to your own life, let the images fall where they may. You may well immerse yourself in daydreams and imagined plans that involve any number of activities that probably cannot be undertaken given the extent of your illness. Imagine them to your heart's delight. Nevertheless, take a nondefensive look at things every now and then. If something is amiss, try to lessen your use of denial so you can see what's happening and better control yourself.

3. Try to stay in touch with the harmful consequences of your denial daydreams and beliefs. In the midst of denial, it is difficult to assess the price paid for this kind of blanket defensiveness. As a rule, the cost is absorbed by the denier and those around him or her, but the situation may become extreme when the denial is acted out in some destructive way. Examples include spending sprees, extended travel, sexual promiscuity, outbursts of violence, and so on. It pays to mix in a measure of insight with your efforts at obliteration.

4. Denial through daydreams is among the safest forms of denial and often safeguards against acting out in ways that are more harmful than otherwise. Escapist daydreams are encouraged.

5. It is then advisable, when faced with a serious illness, to generate as much as possible in the way of positive imagery.

6. Perhaps the greatest danger in denial via daydreams and other means lies with ignoring or rationalizing physical warning signs of pending or actual illness—symptoms that should send you to a doctor in the hope that early detection will give you a longer life or a lasting cure. When denial is invoked in the early stages of an illness, it can be more dangerous than helpful.

Be warned against the use of early denial in any form, such as daydreaming that the symptoms you are experiencing are insignificant or will go away on their own.

If someone you know is using early denial, you should try to puncture that denial and help that person get the medical attention he or she sorely needs.

In principle, early denial daydreams are dangerous, while late-in-the-illness denial daydreams appear to be salutary.

Exercise 8.1

Whether you are ill or not, practice creating positive stories, happy daydreams of any kind. Take a look at the images and themes of these daydreams and notice your own preference for diverting imagery.

In a different vein, take some time to review the events of your day, including your daydreams. How often did you deny or obliterate through imagined stories something you didn't like or didn't want to face or deal with? Can you detect other ways you invoked denial in response to a crisis or concern? Was there any way in which you denied the importance of a physical symptom or psychological/emotional problem?

Comment 8.1

It is advisable to get acquainted with your own denial-based daydreams and see your own preferences for particular types of denial tales—for example, tales of strength and power when you're feeling helpless; of sexual prowess when you're frustrated or threatened; or of immortality when faced with dying.

It also is valuable to discover just how often you—and all of us—invoke denial when under stress. Denial protects us emotionally, but, remember, it precludes other attempts to cope with a problem, including responses that are far more effective in actually changing a situation for the better.

There is a delicate balance between relief through denial and invoking insightful modes of adaptation that can be effective in changing a painful reality into a situation that can be truly mastered.

Denial of Death: An Illustration

Nina is a woman in her mid-50s who has a mammogram and is later told she has a nodule in her breast. She is shocked, distressed, and frightened, but hopeful that the mass is benign. She generates several daydreams in which she imagines that the X-rays showing the nodule were not of her breast, that the radiologist misread her films, and that the nodule will go away on its own. However, she uses the denied embedded in the daydreams to rationalize her delay in seeing the surgeon who was recommended. Her friend Eve realizes she hasn't made the appointment and comes down rather hard on Nina to do so—and Nina finally does.

Denial of illness, supported by all kinds of obliterating daydreams, is extremely common. Few people will consult a doctor at the first sign of a physical problem, and often the delay is even longer with emotional problems. As I said, early denial of illness through daydreams and through any other means is dangerous and can actually lead to the development of a serious illness when early attention to the initial symptoms could have led to a cure. Denial is always costly; sometimes it's worth the price, often it's not.

Nina sees the surgeon, has her surgery, and the nodule is malignant. The doctors also discover she has lymph node involvement and metastases to her bones. The situation is grave, but the doctors offer her hope in the form of a combination of radiation therapy and a new form of chemotherapy.

Despite the many clues that her doctors view the situation as extremely serious, Nina feels optimistic. Her mind is filled with hopeful tales, stories of miracle cures. She automatically and deliberately generates positive daydreams, repeatedly imagining herself traveling here and there, inheriting money, finding a doctor who has cured many cases like hers, and so on. She imagines too that the doctors have made a mistake, that she is already cured and does not really need further treatment, that there's a guru who will heal her body, and that she needn't be concerned about death because she will live on in a spirit world overseen by God.

While somewhat reassuring and serving to reduce her level of anxiety, these daydreams lead Nina to delay seeing her oncologist to arrange for her treatment. One evening, her denial system collapses for a few minutes and she has an involuntary daydream of dying suddenly and with great pain because she's allowed her illness to get out of control. The story prompts Nina to proceed with her treatment.

I will not pursue Nina's story any further, except to note that her use of creative daydream denial helped her through her last days.

Like so much else in nature, denial daydreams can serve you when properly dosed out, yet they can cause harm when overdone. Balancing denial against insight in the face of serious illness is a delicate matter well worth negotiating carefully when called for.

I have taken serious illness and death as my models of major traumas and developed a series of principles related to how to use daydreaming to help you cope with these extreme situations. The same principles apply in general to other kinds of overwhelming events—accidents, injuries, the loss of a job, divorce, and the like. Creative denial is the emergency daydream response and the search for insight the more extended and definitively healing effort. Used properly and wisely, your daydreams can help you to turn a devastating blow into a creative moment that in the long run will give you a more fulfilling life.

CHAPTER 9

Processing the Surface of a Daydream

Having explored the use of daydreams for *creative denial*, it is time to look at the other side of these inventions—their capacity to reflect *meaning* as a potential source of insight. As you may recall, every daydream embodies not one, but two layers of *meaning* within every storyline—one layer directly available on the surface and the other layer encoded by the same surface images.

In principle, when dealing with everyday issues—minor and moderate stresses and traumas—invoking daydreams for creative denial should be a lesser part of your response, and turning to these creations for insight and effective coping strategies should be the greater part. Because we spend so much of our waking lives engaged in this activity, daydreaming must have considerable adaptive value—we mainly need to learn how to gain access to its helpful potentials.

Finding Meaning in Daydreams

There are three ways we can derive meaning from daydream narratives:

1. By looking at and reworking the surface or manifest daydream on its own—the direct daydream images in isolation. This effort

draws upon the conscious system's direct problem-solving capacities as reflected in manifest daydream images.

2.   By discovering a hidden or repressed trigger event that has evoked the daydream response, but is not alluded to in the surface imagery. The repressed trigger is linked with the daydream images and themes revealing adaptive responses to the triggers that are directly expressed in the surface contents of the daydream. In essence, this means:

    a.   You have a problem you are trying to resolve.

    b.   You explore it directly using surface imagery, drawing on the direct resources of the conscious mind—the first type of meaning described above.

    c.   You let go of the problem and have a daydream about something else.

    d.   You then decide to connect this seemingly disconnected daydream to the problem at hand.

    e.   The very act of linking the daydream images to the trigger event yields meaning and insight to which you had not previously had access.

This approach draws upon the capacity of daydreams to reveal *direct but unconscious efforts to solve consciously perceived emotional problems.*

It is time for us to realize that the conscious system of the emotion-processing mind engages in both conscious and unconscious processing. The conscious efforts at adaptation are revealed directly in daydream images that are designed to deal with other problems. The key feature is that of direct revelation, while in contrast, the workings of the deep unconscious system are always revealed indirectly in encoded form.

3.   By taking a daydream, associating its images, and then linking the pool of themes with the trigger events that have evoked them. In this effort, the trigger event may either be stated directly in the daydream or repressed, and therefore alluded to in the daydream only in encoded form.

This is the *use of daydreams for trigger decoding, a process that draws upon the deep unconscious processing of unconsciously perceived trigger events and their meanings.* This is *the second level of meaning* embodied in daydreams and it is very different from the meanings revealed directly in the surface of daydream images. Trigger decoding provides access to our deep unconscious intelligence and its response to unconscious perceptions and experiences.

Directly Fashioned Imagery

We begin our pursuit of meaning and coping strategies with the simplest form of daydreaming: the statement of a problem and the offer of possible answers. Everything is direct and on the surface. This is a most familiar approach to daydreams in that it draws entirely upon the manifest imagery of the daydream to state the issue and imagine possible solutions. The entire effort is transparent and draws solely on conscious system intelligence and wisdom.

This is, then, the classical application of daydreaming to working over emotional and other kinds of problems by imagining and trying out various ways of resolving the dilemmas they pose—using daydreams as thought experiments and as a mental form of trial action.

This first level of meaning that can be extracted from our daydreams involves then:

- A directly stated trigger event.
- A series of directly stated possible solutions to the conflicts and issues the event raises.

Examples of this application of daydreaming are legion. Faced with a choice of jobs, you imagine various aspects of each prospect, conjure up possible contingencies, review the working conditions, anticipate various interactions with other employees and your boss, etc. Or, you are planning to get married and you daydream of what might happen if you decide to go ahead with it or if you decide not to do it.

Faced with choices, anticipated events of all kinds, and consciously recognized conflicts, daydreams are a valuable way of imagining how to work things out, anticipating the consequences of various possibilities, and such. This use of daydreams also is applied to past traumas and stresses, allowing them to be reworked toward insight into what had happened and for generating new solutions to these prior events.

This use of daydreaming is *conscious system problem-solving*—everything is directly stated and reworked entirely within awareness. It draws solely on our direct, conscious intelligence. As such, it can be quite helpful, but it also is rather limited in the resources it can draw on. It's a good way to begin to process a trigger event, but it should be seen only as a first step, followed with trying to access the additional knowledge built into the human mind—indirect forms of conscious intelligence and deep unconscious wisdom.

An Illustration

Donna, a single woman in her late 20s, is lying in bed before going to sleep. She has been dating two men, Howard and David, and feels that it's time to make a choice between them—the situation has been getting too sticky lately. Using small segments of narrative, she goes over the pros and cons of her relationship with each, her likes and dislikes, the emotional and other advantages and disadvantages of the possibility of marrying them—and similar assessments.

Donna then shifts into a more storied mode of thinking and begins to daydream. She recalls a wonderful dinner with Howard at a fine French restaurant and reaches back into other memories, some pleasant and some unpleasant, some with details changed, others faithful to what had happened. She also imagines what life with Howard might be like. He is a successful attorney, and she pictures a house in the suburbs, a summer home, country club life, and a relationship that is stiff and formal.

In one imaginary, spontaneous daydream, she is with Howard at their country club and she meets a man, a new member of the club, who asks her to dance. He's an exciting man and she's attracted to him, but she manages to repel his advances.

Donna now imagines life with David, who is a free-lance writer with an uncertain income, but who has a flair for doing exciting things and is fun to be with. She recalls an unplanned trip they had taken to Atlantic City to do a little gambling and recalls the fun they had. She imagines the future with David, a small apartment, their difficult life together, but this time she pictures herself having a daughter and taking care of her as a newborn and then watching her grow up.

There were, of course, many details to Donna's daydreams as she shifted back and forth in her imagination. For the moment, Donna tentatively decided to break off her relationship with Howard and to continue seeing David. The contrasting daydreams in which she struggled with her fidelity toward Howard and pictured having a baby with David were the critical images that most swayed her toward David. She did, however, also resolve not to do anything until she had time to process her daydreams further so she could delve into her unconscious assessments as well.

In general, when a conflict is severe, conscious choices based on laundry lists and pros and cons thinking often tend to be inconclusive. For every pro for one choice there's a con that counterweighs against it; for every pro or con on one side, there's a pro or con on the other side.

The conscious system is quite poor at making emotionally charged decisions.

On the other hand, the unconscious mind is quite incisive and consistent—with clarity, it will see which side has the most positive features and which is more negative, and it will encode its assessments in well-defined, but camouflaged images. More on that later.

Two Principles for the Direct Use of Daydreams

This first use of daydreams to generate understanding and wise adaptive choices is fairly straightforward and largely a matter of catching the messages you've imparted to yourself. The following can serve as guiding principles:

- Whenever you are confronted with a notable emotionally tinged decision or choice, be sure to use your daydreams as part of your effort to reach sound conclusions.

- The first approach should be quite direct. Take the situation, think it through, and then take a straight route and daydream about the different sides of the decision. This will give you additional access to your conscious thinking about the matter. The shift is from directly weighing the pros and cons, to directly weighing the situation via narratives. This brings two different modes of direct conscious system thinking and intelligence to the issues.

The Breakthrough Surface Insight

In addition to the understanding that emerges through conscious deliberations, there is a second way you may directly achieve conscious understanding of a conflict or issue you are working over. This happens when an insight suddenly comes to mind, emerging whole cloth from your imagination as you rework the problem at hand. Often, this understanding materializes through a daydream image, but it may pop into your head at any time.

These emergent images and insights come from the unconscious part of the conscious mind, in that they do not develop on the basis of logical arguments, but break through from a part of the mind that operates without awareness. We know that we store many memories in an unconscious part of the conscious mind, memories that are readily brought into awareness in their direct form. This same unconscious system—it is called *the superficial unconscious subsystem of the conscious mind*—also has some processing capabilities.

This means that while you were consciously working over an emotional problem, the unconscious part of your conscious mind has also been doing the same without your knowledge. Suddenly, this system chooses to speak and its insight breaks through into awareness. It's a conscious system insight in that it is expressed directly and without disguise. And it usually is of a different order from the understanding you've achieved through conscious reasoning—and well worth adding to your conscious assessment of the situation.

Remarkably enough, then, when faced with an emotional problem, your mind reworks it in three ways—consciously, through direct deliberations; unconsciously, through relevant conscious experience without immediate awareness; and deeply unconsciously, through relevant unconscious experience.

Donna soon came back to her decision regarding Howard and David. Still feeling unsettled, in her mind she repeated the pros and cons of each man, adding only a few minor details. But this time, as she was going back and forth, she suddenly remembered an incident with Howard that she had forgotten entirely. It took place when they first met and Donna had rationalized it at the time and, without realizing it, had repressed it until now.

Soon after meeting Howard, Donna fell ill with a gastrointestinal virus. She lives alone and was quite ill in bed when Howard happened to call to see if they could get together. Donna desperately needed some medicine and supplies, and she eventually asked Howard, who worked nearby, if he could help. Howard responded with a flood of reasons why he wasn't available at the moment and wouldn't be until late that night.

Donna accepted his excuses at the time, but now, as she suddenly recalled this incident, she felt Howard should have come through for her. He's a withholding man, she thought now, he won't be there for me when I need him. The breakthrough story confirmed her assessment that breaking up with Howard was the right thing to do.

We'll hear more about Donna in the next chapter. For now, let's summarize and realize again that the *conscious mind* operates through deliberations done with full awareness, but it also has *its own superficial unconscious processing system.* The hallmark of this latter kind of intelligence is that its knowledge and insights are conveyed directly and without disguise in your daydreams and thoughts.

This includes sudden conscious realizations that can readily be integrated into your conscious thinking.

So much for our surface daydream images, our conscious intelligence, and consciously coping with our emotionally charged trigger events. The surface of a daydream is a wise place to start your processing, but an unwise place to end it. So let's move on to deeper realms.

CHAPTER 10

Daydreams and Unconscious Processing

We are moving into the realm of unconscious experience and the role that daydreams play in enabling us to access the brilliant intelligence and coping skills that operate in the deep unconscious system of the mind.

Two Perspectives

It will help to orient ourselves at the outset of this part of our journey by developing two perspectives.

1. Until you have spent a good deal of time trigger decoding your daydreams and learning the ins and outs of the emotion-processing mind, it is impossible to appreciate how much of our lives we live out in the wrong place and with the wrong people, making the wrong decisions for the wrong reasons—and suffering for it all.

What I mean by this is, as we will soon see, the human mind has evolved with a preference to avoiding disturbing emotional confrontations, to repressing many of its hurtful experiences, to using self-harm to control our anger and rage at others, and to maintaining idols and heroes at all costs. These factors have configured our minds to automatically deny and repress many of the hurts done to us by those whom we love or revere or need, and to *displace our actions elsewhere.*

This displacement spares us much anxiety and preserves relation-ships that we believe we need to maintain, doing so largely because we deny and repress their hurtful qualities. But at the same time, dis-placement causes us to react to others who essentially have not harmed us, responding to them as if they had done us damage (which was done, however, by another party). We find ways to pick quarrels, to justify misplaced anger, to rationalize hurting these displaced vic-tims of our *unconscious* defenses and needs, and to otherwise damage suitable relationships to preserve harmful ones we cannot bear to consciously see as harmful or ones we cannot surrender.

In opting for as much as possible in the way of denial and repres-sion—for defensiveness rather than insight—evolution has given us an emotion-processing mind much in need of repair and help.

The trigger decoding we're about to develop is exactly the help we need.

Trigger decoding is the only known way to set things right and face the truth around us—and benefit accordingly. It's the only means we have for accessing our highly accurate unconscious perceptions of the world—both others and ourselves—in place of the highly dis-torted and erroneous perceptions we experience consciously. Given nature's design, we're a lot better off when we do so.

We need to trigger decode our daydreams practically every day if we want to correct our natural tendency to see the world other than it really is.

2.   Secondly, we want to be reminded that we have two kinds of basic intelligence when it comes to dealing with or processing emotionally charged information and meaning. The first is developed through *the conscious system of the emotion processing mind* and involves all levels of intelligence that can reach awareness in direct and comprehensible form, including, as we just saw, direct and knowing deliberations as well as superficial unconscious processing that can break through into awareness directly in one form or another.

The second basic intelligence operates entirely outside of awareness and is part of *the deep unconscious system of the emotion-processing mind*. It operates from beginning (perception) to end (communication) *entirely outside of awareness*, never revealing itself through a manifest or direct image. Trigger decoding your daydreams is the only way you can access this deep intelligence.

Keep in mind that:

a. Deep unconscious intelligence and processing operates in a very different way than the more familiar conscious intelligence and it arrives at very different and far more valid and helpful conclusions.

   The conscious and deep unconscious realms of experience are worlds apart.

b. In general, the more your insights stem from the deep unconscious part of the mind, the more informative and useful they are likely to be—conscious intelligence is very limited in the emotional world.

c. We process all emotionally charged trigger events with two distinctive mental systems. While the conscious system determines our adaptive behaviors, the deep unconscious system in a sense knows better. Trigger decoding is the means by which we bring this wiser knowledge into awareness, affording it a say in our actual coping responses.

d. The conscious system has its own unconscious subsystem, the superficial unconscious subsystem, which stores directly accessible, consciously registered information and meaning that also processes consciously registered emotional inputs.

   The deep unconscious system stores and processes all subliminally perceived information and meaning, and has its own deep wisdom subsystem.

In all then, we have both conscious and deeply unconscious systems of intelligence. Our conscious intelligence is twofold, with both conscious and unconscious processors, while our deep unconscious intelligence is singular and always operates outside of awareness.

Accessing Deep Unconscious Intelligence

With these perspectives, we can continue our exploration of how to access and use the wisdom of the emotion-processing mind. We shift now to a system that *can communicate only through encoded messages*—the deep unconscious system. We turn to this system with a lot of advance publicity—I've been stressing its capacity to see people and events as they truly are and to process what we experience outside of awareness with profound insight. I've also tried to show that living our lives without its wisdom entails considerable unneeded pain and suffering, while accessing its wise ways, though often disturbing, promises each of us a far better life.

Two Types of Trigger Decoding

Trigger decoding daydream imagery takes two forms.

The first form, which I will describe in this chapter, is relatively straightforward. It is carried out with a consciously identified trigger event and a displaced daydream story—one that involves imagery that is manifestly unrelated to the trigger situation.

The two components are then a trigger and a disguised daydream. Decoding is accomplished by linking the themes in the daydream story to the trigger event, shaped to reveal deep unconscious perceptions and insights.

The second form is more complex in that it deals with both known and unknown or repressed triggers, and entails the build up of a thematic pool through associations to the elements of a daydream story. We will rework this all-purpose approach to the deep unconscious mind and its adaptive wisdom in the final part of this book.

The Essential Steps in Trigger Decoding

In trigger decoding, we are trying to access our own deep unconscious wisdom as activated by an emotionally charged trigger event. The human mind is designed first, to encode its strongest reactions to triggers, and second, to keep these encoded images separate from the trigger events to which they are responsive. Trigger decoding undoes both of these natural defenses, thereby revealing unconsciously perceived truths that can constructively guide our emotionally related choices and concerns.

The key steps in trigger decoding are:

1. Having a daydream (and in the second form, associating to its elements).
2. Extracting the themes in the daydream.
3. Discovering an activated trigger event.
4. Linking the themes to the trigger.
5. Creating a narrative of adaptation that begins with the trigger event and treats the themes as reflections of valid unconscious perceptions of the meanings of the trigger.
6. Identifying and using the coping strategies encoded in the themes of the daydream as they pertain to the trigger event.

Little by little, I want to help you understand exactly what each of these steps entails.

The Basic Form Trigger Decoding

The first approach to trigger decoding may involve either of two sequences.

In the first sequence, you begin with a known trigger event and move on to the relevant daydream themes, while in the second sequence, you begin with the daydream themes and find a suitable trigger event. Let's see how they work.

The *first sequence* goes like this:

1. Identify an active emotionally charged trigger event.
2. Harvest your spontaneous daydreams from earlier in the day.
3. Add to these stories at least one—and preferably several— freely woven daydream stories made up at the moment.
4. Harvest all of the themes that do *not* refer directly to the trigger event. These are your encoded themes.
5. Identify and collate these themes.

6. Detach these themes from their manifest daydream story, giving you an extracted *narrative pool or pool of themes.*

7. Take the trigger event and link it to the themes in the narrative pool.

8. Read out the connections between the trigger and the themes as a cause-and-effect sequence.

9. Shape this readout into a story of adaptation. It should begin with the trigger event and move to your decoded valid unconscious perceptions of its meanings.

10. Look for encoded suggestions as to how the trigger event should be handled or adapted to.

11. Heed the perceptions and adaptive strategies emanating from your deep unconscious mind in deciding how to deal with the trigger event.

The displaced themes in your daydream pool reflect your deep unconscious view of the trigger situation. They convey a realistic picture whose features you have selected according to your own issues and needs.

Encoded themes reflect personally selected, but highly valid (nondistorted) pictures of trigger situations.

The *second sequence* of basic trigger decoding begins with the themes in a daydream pool of images, instead of with a known trigger event. Once the pool of themes has been established, you search for a critical trigger event that is compatible with the pool of themes. The essence of what follows is similar to the sequence you use when you begin with the trigger event. It too culminates in linking the trigger to the themes as valid encoded perceptions of that event.

The essential feature of basic trigger decoding is that you connect displaced/encoded themes in the manifest pool of daydream images with a single, active trigger event—there is no further trigger search and no effort to associate to the daydream images.

It's time to see these modes of trigger decoding in action—it will make the process a lot clearer.

Returning to the Story of Donna

We return to Donna and her decision about Howard and David. Donna grew tired of her deliberations and decided to let go of them for a while. She laid back and allowed her mind to wander and create its own daydream. Quite soon she was imagining her friend Teresa and Teresa's old boyfriend, Jimmy. She began to recall an incident in which Jimmy, who was an artist, was evicted from his apartment because he couldn't pay his rent. Partly from memory and partly from imagination, Donna envisioned a scene between Teresa and Jimmy, where Jimmy wanted to live with Teresa and Teresa raised objections to the idea. Jimmy got violent and cornered Teresa, and threatened to hit her, but Teresa escaped the apartment and called the police, who saw to it that Jimmy left and promised not to return.

Question 10.1

Connect this partly borrowed, partly made up, daydream to the trigger situation. What does this thinly disguised story tell you about Donna's unconscious perception of one of her present boyfriends? Which one is portrayed in slightly disguised fashion in this story? Why did you select whomever you chose? Also, what is the encoded advice that Donna gives to herself through this daydream?

Answer 10.1

Stories of this kind, which are readily connected to trigger events, give us an opportunity to appreciate the ways in which the unconscious mind encodes and represents the realities it experiences—and recommends adaptive responses as well.

Donna had consciously dropped the emotionally charged choice she was exploring—Howard and David are her triggers. She then generated a daydream that *on the surface (consciously)* was unrelated to the problem. However, knowing how the emotion-processing mind works, we can be certain that on the *encoded level (unconsciously),* the daydream themes are very much related to the trigger event.

Whenever your mind relaxes and begins to think about something else in narrative form, the deep unconscious mind influences the creative center to weave a story that encodes reactions to the trigger events you are reworking at the moment.

With Donna, we have the themes and we know the trigger. All we need to do now is link the themes in the displaced, encoded story to the emotional debate in which Donna is engaged. In doing so, we begin with the *bridging images*—the themes that are shared by the meanings of the trigger event and the daydream story—to establish the link between the trigger and the themes.

It seems evident that Jimmy, who is an unemployed artist, represents—stands in for—David, who is an unemployed, free-lance, writer. The shared themes are unemployment and artistry—Jimmy is an available stand-in or a representation of David.

This unconscious use of displacement is one of the essential means by which the human mind—the deep unconscious system and the unconscious creative center—fashions its encoded stories. David is displaced onto and represented by Jimmy; a person (Jimmy) who shares a feature with a trigger-related individual (David) is used to represent that individual.

Through this mechanism, there is no awareness of who the daydream is about unless the displacement is undone. And this unmasking is possible in definitive fashion only in light of the trigger event.

Any other approach involves arbitrary guesswork.

With the bridges established, we next connect the themes of the daydream with the trigger event. We do this in simple terms, as decoded perceptions of the trigger experience. That is, we treat this story as Donna's *valid,* unconscious view of David—the nondefensive truth about David, so to speak. And we make this statement in the form of an *adaptational narrative*—this is how Donna sees David, and this is what she should do about him in light of what she sees.

Thus, we would propose that Donna is unconsciously working over her unconscious perceptions of David as an unemployed writer. She envisions his being destitute, being asked to leave his apartment for nonpayment of his rent, wanting to live with her, and becoming violent when she puts him off. Indeed, asking him to leave and getting help from the police to get him to do so is the main *adaptive recommendation* from her deep unconscious system: drop him—he's unreliable, angry, and trouble.

This *decoded story* reflects perceptions of David that had not emerged consciously from Donna's more direct analysis, musings, and conscious elements of her daydreams. The perception comes from a nonconscious intelligence—a deep unconscious intelligence that is far more perceptive, nondefensive, and blunt than our conscious vision and intelligence.

As you may recall, consciously, Donna was favoring sustaining her relationship with David rather than Howard. Now, her deep unconscious mind is telling her to drop David. Which part of her mind is right?

In almost all instances, you will discover that greater wisdom and better coping strategies are reflected in the encoded rather than the direct response.

Summing Up the Process

Let's now put together the trigger decoding process we just saw in action. The steps were:

1. Finding an active trigger event—David's wanting to be with Donna.
2. Having a displaced daydream about something else—the imagined story about Teresa and Jimmy.
3. Extracting the main themes from the daydream narrative— someone who is destitute, unreliable, invasive, overly needy, a loser, and trouble.
4. Linking these themes to the trigger event as valid decoded perceptions—David is destitute, unreliable, invasive, overly needy, a loser, and trouble.

5. Finding an adaptive strategy encoded in the displaced day-dream—get rid of David.
   And, as we're about to see:
6. Validating your interpretation or impressions of these efforts by trigger decoding a fresh daydream story.
7. Discovering repressed memories, adding further validating imagery, reworking your conscious view of the trigger situation, and coming to a suitable decision.

The Follow-up

Deciding which part of yourself—conscious or unconscious—to believe depends on both a further conscious reworking of the issues in light of the messages you have trigger decoded, and on the generation of a fresh daydream that can then be examined for validating imagery.

Alerted by these images, a flood of repressed memories came back to Donna and they were in keeping with her encoded picture of David. There were recollections of a time when David's electricity and telephone were shut off because he hadn't paid his bills, and of a time when he came to Donna's apartment in the middle of the night because his landlord had locked him out of his apartment for not paying the rent. Donna was furious at the intrusion, but allowed David to sleep on her living room couch, always regretting having done it because David later became intrusive in other ways. Donna was quite amazed that she had repressed these unfavorable recollections, but that's exactly what her conscious mind had done.

Next, Donna developed a fresh daydream to see if the images confirmed or failed to support this new view of David. The story was brief. It was about a man who works in Donna's office, who people view as friendly and nice. Donna imagined him losing control with his secretary and slapping her face.

Question 10.2

Which of Donna's assessments of David—conscious or unconscious—does this story support? Explain the basis for your answer.

Answer 10.2

Incorporating these themes into her trigger situation, it would appear that Donna's deep unconscious mind is saying that David may look good at first (conscious) glance, but the truth is he's nasty and ill-tempered. Clearly, *her deep unconscious appraisal* is the one that finds support here.

Still puzzled over this unexpected image, Donna associated briefly to the man. She realized that while he seemed very nice on the surface, it was well-known in their office that he had a bad temper and had tried to seduce several women in the office. He had asked Donna out and she had wisely refused him.

Confirming Your Formulation

Once you have interpreted your daydream images in light of a trigger event, it is essential to generate and process a fresh daydream narrative and decode its themes to determine if they do or do not support your formulation. If they do not, be prepared to go back over your effort to seek either a different and more cogent trigger event, or a fresh interpretation of your themes in light of the trigger with which you are working.

Donna's pool of fresh daydream themes clearly validated her impressions of her previous daydream images and their decoded messages. We can say this because the new pool of themes echoed the earlier themes—they involved a man who has a violent temper, who can't be trusted, and who is to be refused when he asks for a date.

Validation of this kind led Donna to take her unconscious wisdom very seriously, all the more so because she now suddenly remembered another story that a friend who knew David told her—something she also had completely forgotten (repressed). The friend knew a woman David had dated who told the friend that David had terrible fits of temper and could get violent when he was overly frustrated.

You may be surprised at how much Donna had repressed regarding David. But I assure you this is how the conscious mind is designed—to forget rather than remember, to be ignorant rather than knowledgeable, to allow hurt to occur rather than protect us emotionally. Again, this is why we need to trigger decode our daydreams—the deep unconscious mind does not share these costly defensive needs.

In principle, if you have interpreted your daydream images in light of a given trigger, decoding the next set of daydream images in light of the same trigger should produce encoded stories that confirm your formulations. In addition, it should help you remove many conscious system repressive barriers and bring forth forgotten memories—incidents that have been buried because they are too painful to recall and because, unfortunately, their repression serves our unconscious need to suffer.

The Last Piece

There's a surprising postscript to Donna's story. After working through her picture of David, it suddenly occurred to her that throughout his college years, Howard had been a painter—a house painter. This meant that through the mechanism of *condensation*, another vital mechanism that we will soon explore, Jimmy also represented or stood for Howard.

This realization led Donna to unearth a number of problems with Howard that she also had repressed. A fresh daydream about a physician friend whose wife recently divorced him and who also stood in for Howard—both are professionals—appeared to validate the fresh doubts about him that Donna was now experiencing.

When she was done reworking this side, she understood why she'd been so depressed over the last months. She was in two relationships that were not only unsatisfying, but at times quite hurtful. With further daydream processing and thought, Donna decided to break up with both men. Although the experience was decidedly painful, she found herself with a new lease on life and soon met a man who proved to be far more loving and nonconflictual than either David or Howard. Happy endings are common after trigger decoding.

Summing Up

It takes some effort to develop the skill of bringing encoded daydream themes to their trigger events. But doing so gives voice to your own inner genius in the world of emotions—your best possible ally in this realm. In a social world where emotional suffering and misguided emotionally charged choices are myriad, making use of this hidden genius is essential for a satisfying life. With this in mind, let's turn now to the more elaborate method of trigger decoding that brings us most intensely in touch with our own deep wisdom and its wonderfully adaptive directives.

CHAPTER 11

Daydreams and Disguise

We are about to enter full force a world of unconscious experience that is awesome, extremely powerful in its silent influence over our lives, and very different from our world of conscious experience. We are indeed, as neuroscientists have suggested, not only of two *brains,* right and left, but also of two *minds.* But contrary to brain-based expectations, we do not possess a global emotion-processing mind on one level and a logical, reasoning mind on the other. Indeed, one of the great surprises to arise from trigger decoding both dreams and daydreams is the discovery of two logical, reasoning systems of the mind—one potentially conscious, the other deeply unconscious.

What then are the main differences and similarities between the conscious and deep unconscious systems of the mind? Identifying these distinguishing features will help us get acquainted with a level of experience that we can fathom only indirectly, mainly by trigger decoding our daydreams. Failing that, we live in complete ignorance of half of our lives, a half that has far more power in the emotional realm than the half with which we're familiar.

The Two Systems of the Mind

The main differences and similarities between the conscious and unconscious systems of the mind are:

1. Both systems receive information and meaning through our senses, especially our eyes and ears, and both have an intelligence that uses reasoning and logic in their operations. However, the conscious system receives consciously registered inputs, while the deep unconscious system receives subliminal or unconsciously registered inputs. The result is two very separate and distinctive processing pathways.

2. The conscious system has *broad vision* and is capable of seeing everything, even though, because of its pervasive defensiveness, it misses a great deal. On the other hand, the vision of the deep unconscious system is primarily concentrated on ground-rule and frame/contextual issues, and secondarily, on whether its communications are being understood and whether a person is being helpful or hurtful. In all, the deep unconscious system is a frame-focused system, while the conscious system is only vaguely concerned with such issues.

3. On the expressive side, the conscious system communicates via surface/manifest messages and these vary from stories of all kinds to a variety of intellectual expressions such as analysis, descriptions, ideas, and the like. The meanings expressed are direct—what is said is what is meant, including the implications of what has been said. The system also is limited to expressing one thought at a time in a linear, logical sequence.

   On the other hand, the deep unconscious system communicates almost entirely through narrative messages. The resultant images are, however, *displaced and condensed*—what is said may stand for itself, but it mainly stands for several other things simultaneously. This means communication is always in the form of multiple, simultaneous, disguised messages. Because of its capabilities for multiple representations, this system can say a lot more in far less time than can the conscious system.

4. The conscious system is geared toward personal survival. It needs to function in terms of direct experience and without symbols so it can cope with real danger and find the real means of surviving. However, because there are so many survival

issues to negotiate and because our worlds and social interactions are so complex and demanding, the conscious system has little energy for nonsurvival emotional issues—of which there are a multitude.

As a result of these factors, the conscious system is safeguarded by its massive defensiveness in respect to emotionally charged impingements. The system has built-in perceptual defenses and automatically shunts a large part of the incoming emotionally charged stimuli to unconscious rather than conscious perception.

All in all, our conscious system processing capacities in respect to emotional events—our conscious emotionally-related IQ's—are quite restricted. In addition, as noted earlier, the use of self-punishment to curtail conscious inclinations toward violence against others renders this system treacherous and unreliable in the emotional realm. This arrangement probably evolved to constrain the enormous amount of violence we harbor within our minds as reflected subtly or grossly in our actions—anger and rage caused by countless frustrations, physical and psychological assaults from others, damaging events, and the awareness of the eventuality of personal death.

With this as our perspective, let's turn our attention to the deep unconscious system and, in particular, to how daydreams are created. Insight into this remarkable process will enable us to learn the details of the second and most complete method of trigger decoding our daydream narratives.

The Creation of an Encoded Daydream

Every daydream is constructed by a *deeply unconscious creative center* with roots in both the conscious and unconscious systems of the mind. We can consciously and deliberately determine the course of a daydream, but even as we do so, our imagination is influenced by two unconscious systems—the unconscious subsystem of the conscious mind and the deep unconscious subsystem of the unconscious mind.

Under mandates from both conscious and unconscious experience then, the creative center must invent a story that will satisfy our conscious intentions while at the same time satisfy our unconscious needs to convey, in encoded form, the results of the unconscious processing of important trigger events. The complexity of the task staggers the imagination and speaks for one of the most remarkable and unappreciated feats of nature.

In essence, a manifest daydream is a product of an inner creative center that is under the simultaneous influence of conscious and deep unconscious forces. A daydream is one of the most miraculous creations of the human mind.

A daydream is a two–tiered communication, a direct statement and a transformed narrative—a camouflaged story whose encoded messages are disguised within the direct statement. The encoded messages in daydreams are so plentiful (we have a lot to rework emotionally each day), and so powerful and potentially disturbing that evolution has provided us with two remarkable, yet basically uncomplicated, mechanisms—displacement and condensation—with which to fashion the encoded aspect of every daydream image. Both mechanisms operate automatically and unconsciously whenever we create a daydream story.

The human mind makes use of narrative language as a coded statement that, like any good code, tells a surface tale while expressing a second disguised and more powerful tale. Instead of the dots and dashes of the Morse code where dot, dot, dot means just that, but also means the letter "S," the inventive human mind uses surface stories as its dots and dashes, and encodes its second story by that means.

While dots lack meaning, the letters they represent can convey meaning; the human code uses meaning to encode meaning.

Displacement

The first mechanism of encoding is called *disguise through displacement* and it is the backbone of encoded human communication. By means of displacement, one thing is represented by another thing—person, place, event, and such. Displacement is fundamental to the use of symbols and all forms of disguise.

There has been a tendency to think of displacement as a mental mechanism by which the human mind creates symbols designed for inner expression. I must therefore stress that:

Displacement is an adaptive mechanism that is invoked to disguise our painful unconscious responses to emotionally charged trigger events.

We unconsciously perceive something quite anxiety-provoking, process it outside of our awareness, and then, by virtue of the basic design of the human mind and how it expresses itself or communicates with ourselves and others, we portray or represent what we have experienced through an image that is different from the experience itself.

The representative or displaced image is chosen because it shares attributes with the original perception, while simultaneously disguising it as well.

In the vignette with Donna that we've been exploring, David was represented through displacement by Jimmy, and so was Howard. Donna's apartment was displaced onto Teresa's apartment—and so on.

To clarify these ideas, consider the following:

1. The world of unconscious experience is a straightforward, very logical world, with candid perceptiveness, a sense of the truly primitive qualities of human behaviors, messages, and experiences. It is highly rational and intelligent in its processing capacities, and enormously inventive in its communicative capabilities. It is not simply a wildly irrational, uncontrolled world—those qualities accrue to the conscious world and our knowing behaviors and the drive-related, impulsive aspects of the conscious and unconscious parts of the mind.

2. The strangeness of the unconscious world comes from the means by which evolution constrains its means of expressing itself. That is, it can communicate with the outside world only through displaced images—only via indirection and encoded narratives.

3. In practical terms, to appreciate the ways of this world and to
benefit from its great wisdom, you need to think as your
unconscious mind thinks. This means that almost nothing is
what it seems; everything stands for something else—and as we
shall soon see, stands for several other things at once. Nothing
can be taken at face value. A surface message is another message, not itself, but some other thing.

However, trying to figure out—to decode—the second meanings of a daydream's surface message is not a guessing game.
These disguised meanings are responses to emotionally
charged trigger events. Once you know the trigger, you can
accurately unmask the disguise. Without the trigger you are
pretty much in a quandary—you are faced with many seemingly disconnected themes in need of an organizer to provide
specific meaning. The trigger is the Rosetta stone to the hiero-
glyphic language of human encoding—it is the key to unlock-
ing the mystery of the second set of meanings which have been
definitively shaped by a specific trigger event.

To offer a brief example, Abner has a daydream about his office-
mate, a man, who is being tied to a chair and whipped by a woman
dressed in black. Another man comes into the room and stops the
whipping.

Question 11.1

*Propose at least two trigger events to which this daydream could
be a displaced, encoded response. Remember that the themes in the
daydream link up with attributes or meanings of the trigger experience. Once you pick the two triggers, notice how each shapes the
encoded meanings in this brief story.*

Answer 11.1

The trigger event for this daydream could be any situation in
which Abner has been trapped or constrained and harmed. Someone

is freeing Abner as well. In this case, Abner's office-mate is displaced from and represents Abner.

To cite some possibilities, the trigger could be an incident in which Abner's wife insisted he come home to dinner instead of going drinking with his buddies from work. In this instance, the daydream encodes Abner's feelings of entrapment and harm in her demand. The man represents his buddies whom he hopes will rescue him from his plight.

But the trigger event for this daydream also could be an affair that Abner is having with a woman from work, in which she has decided to stop seeing Abner because she's become involved with another man. Here, it is the woman who feels trapped and damaged because Abner has not kept his promise to leave his wife for her. Through displacement, Abner's office-mate represents the woman and the other man represents the woman's new boyfriend—he's rescuing her from Abner.

The daydream also could be a response to a trigger event in which Abner had a car accident, was trapped momentarily in his car, and was rescued by a passing motorist.

Actually, the daydream was a response to all three trigger events and the images take on all three sets of meanings depending on which trigger you link the daydream images to. The same images can represent an infinite number of possible triggers and meanings. This introduces us to the second major mechanism the human mind uses in encoding a daydream story—*condensation.*

Condensation

The second means of encoding is called *disguise through condensation.* Every daydream element we imagine—every narrative image our minds create—actually represents two or more (usually several) different persons, places, or events. Primarily, this is because *each element combines reactions to two or more distinctive trigger events.* So, remarkably enough, the automatic use of displacement is constrained by requisites for using images that serve condensation. That is, the creative center must comply with three requisites in creating a daydream story. It must:

1. Fashion a consciously determined set of surface images into a coherent story.
2. Use images in the story that also encode, via displacement, an unconscious message regarding a recognized or unrecognized trigger event.
3. Use images that also satisfy the requirement for condensation, that is, to create a story that simultaneously stands for two or more encoded messages related to two or more trigger events.

In essence, then, displacement is carried out under the constraints of condensation.

To clarify further, we have already seen that a daydream element stands for itself—its surface contents—and for a disguised message. But condensation sees to it that the element actually disguises several different messages rather than a single message. Each daydream element is a layered, simultaneous response to several critical trigger events.

While conscious communication is single meaning in nature—a rose is a rose is a rose—deep unconscious communication is multiple meaning—a rose is a friend, an enemy, a lover, and whoever else.

Remarkably, then, conscious communication occurs in a straight line, one message at a time, while unconscious communication proceeds with several messages at once. The latter is clearly a more effective way of expressing oneself. Indeed, given the multiplicity of strong trigger events we experience each day, the conscious mind could not conceivably process all of them, while the deep unconscious mind certainly could—and does.

The way we reveal the operation of condensation is by associating to daydream elements and then discovering the different trigger events for the resultant pool of themes.

These associated stories reveal the different persons, places, and events that have been encoded into each daydream element, and the triggers to which these elements are a response. Once the various triggers are known, the fact that the daydream encodes reactions to each trigger event becomes apparent.

Question 11.2

Think back to the vignette about Donna, described in the previous chapter. Where can we see condensation in operation? Go back to the story about Abner—where is condensation operating there?

Answer 11.2

In the vignette about Donna, it was through condensation that Jimmy stood for both David and Howard—as we discovered through Donna's associations to her daydream. In terms of trigger events, this means that incidents with each of them had triggered her daydream images.

As for Abner's daydream, it condensed responses to three different trigger events—that with his wife, his mistress, and the car accident.

It takes some getting used to, but the human brain is the most complex matter system in the universe. We should not be surprised with its remarkable mental capabilities.

The Adaptive Sequence

Much like night dreams, a daydream is the end point of an adaptive sequence that begins with a trigger event and culminates in the two-tiered communicative narrative response—the daydream images—as well as other reactions, many of them behavioral. In working with and decoding daydreams, we actually are starting with the end of this sequence of happenings—with the results of conscious and unconscious processing and mental coping efforts that have been evoked by a trigger event.

This means that in decoding our daydreams we must begin with the themes and work our way back to the trigger event that evoked them. This enables us to decode and understand the insights and coping strategies that are camouflaged in the daydream images.

Fundamentally, we are dealing with the efforts of the human mind—specifically, those parts of the mind that have evolved to cope with emotionally charged information and meaning, *the emotion-processing mind*—to adapt to emotionally charged trigger events. The sequence, as it occurs over time, is the following:

1.   The emotionally charged trigger event.

2.   The conscious perception and experience of aspects of that event, coupled with the simultaneous unconscious perception and experience of different, more threatening and often frame-related aspects of the same event.

3.   The conscious processing of the consciously registered aspects of the trigger event, their surface meanings and implications. Simultaneously, the unconscious processing of the unconsciously registered aspects of the trigger event, their meanings and implications.

As for the steps in the above sequence, we should review and elaborate the following considerations:

   a.   We process the total experience of a trigger event using two systems of the mind—the conscious system and the deep unconscious system.

   b.   The means of processing this information and meaning is called our intelligence, and it embodies a constellation of analyzing and coping skills.

   c.   We possess two very different kinds of intelligence. The first is part of the conscious system and is reflected in our conscious deliberations related to the trigger event—our conscious adaptive efforts and skills. The second is part of the deep unconscious system and it operates entirely outside of awareness.

   d.   In the emotional realm, our conscious capacities to deal with emotionally charged trigger events is minimal, relatively ineffectual, and often inherently self-defeating. The conscious system is primarily a survival-directed system with little energy for dealing with emotional issues that do not immediately pose a threat to one's life. It also is a system under the strong control of unconscious guilt and need for self-punishment.

   e.   In principle, when dealing with an emotionally charged event, issue, or decision, we are well-advised to take our conscious deliberations and choices with a great deal of caution. We should turn to our unconscious deliberations and choices for sound and effective answers—a step that requires the use of *trigger decoding*, the deciphering of disguised meanings in day-dream images in light of the trigger events that evoked them.

f. The intelligence capacities of the deep unconscious system, which develop through subliminal perceptions and unconscious experiences from childhood on, are highly skilled and incisive in their abilities to process unconsciously perceived information and meaning, and arrive at sound and highly valuable adaptive solutions.

g. While the conscious system's purview and vision is spread out over many dimensions of human experience, the vision of the deep unconscious system is concentrated on laws, rules, and boundaries—ground rules or frames.

4. Once a trigger event has been processed within awareness, we usually arrive at some conscious conclusions and decide how to respond—cope with or adapt to the event. This response involves both thought and action—the conscious system is responsible for and controls our conscious thoughts, behaviors, and feelings. However, unconscious influence is ever-present.

> *Whatever the unknown, unconscious influences on conscious functioning—and there are many—it is well to realize that conscious deliberations are known to us directly and lead us to conscious adaptive decisions.*

There also is simultaneous, unconscious processing of the same trigger event, with adaptive solutions proposed by the deep unconscious system. These wiser choices *never surface or break through directly into awareness*; by virtue of the design of the mind, they cannot be directly stated. To anthropomorphize once more for clarity, all our deep unconscious intelligence can do is pass its deliberations on to the unconscious creative center that receives this information and encodes it into the surface images of the daydream.

The encoded narratives that make up our daydreams, and the encoded stories that are condensed into each element of a daydream, are the means by which the unconscious mind tells us what it's been doing. Daydreams are a vehicle through which the deep unconscious mind reaches the surface or manifest contents of our thinking, though always in encoded form.

This arrangement reflects a compromise in the design of the emotion processing mind that makes decoding your daydreams such a critical and health-giving effort. The human mind possesses a deep and effective unconscious intelligence, *but that intelligence has no direct outlet into awareness and no direct effect on our adaptive solutions and actions.* The only known way to bring this intelligence to bear on conscious emotional choices is through trigger decoding, to decipher the disguised messages emitted by this deep intelligence.

The daydream is, then, an encoded resource. Its storyline and the associations to its elements encode our unconscious experience and the processing of the nonconscious or repressed aspects of the emotionally charged impingements with which we must cope day after day. It is insufficient to simply read out the implications of the surface of a daydream or to connect it in some vague way to a trigger event. The human mind reacts to specific events and their specific meanings.

Enriching the Daydream Network

Until now, I have been speaking only of the daydream itself, without elaboration. I must now introduce a vital addendum. We are compelled to deal with so many trigger events each day, each with so many complex meanings, that it is impossible to encode all of our unconscious perceptions and reactions to these perceptions in a day's yield of daydream stories.

Evolution has taken care of this communicative need through the aforementioned mechanism of condensation. When the creative center forms a daydream story, it uses condensation to pack into each detail or element of the story two or more additional stories that encode additional reactions to the trigger events with which the unconscious mind is coping. Each of these encoded stories contributes markers to the daydream detail which, in turn, like the proverbial tip of the iceberg, represents each of these stories—one tip or daydream element standing for several underlying narratives. In this way, the daydream is like a dry sponge, awaiting associations to its elements to fill out its vast potential of storied material.

Through condensation, reactions to multiple triggers and their multiple meanings are conveyed in brief daydream stories. To unpack these marked and represented narratives, all we need to do is associate to a fresh story in response to each detail or element of a given daydream. This process is called *guided associating* and we will soon study it in detail. For now, let's establish the principle that:

> *Daydreams are created to be associated to so you can build a*
> *rich narrative pool that is then available for decoding in light of*
> *the many trigger events that evoked that pool.*

The richness of this pool of themes, once linked to its triggers, enables you to get in touch consciously with your own deep wisdom and the best possible solutions to your various emotional concerns—and to use the knowledge so gained in coping with each.

The process that begins with an emotional trigger can end satisfactorily only with a trigger-decoded insight. On this level, all else is compromise, and doing less deprives you of the use of your own deep and incisive wisdom. You leave yourself at the mercy of the often self-hurtful, unconscious powers that govern much of your conscious emotional life—all to the worse rather than the better.

Strange, indeed, is the design of the emotion-processing mind. Evolved in this fashion to spare us the enormous pain of the implications of many of our own behaviors, and the actions of those we love and with whom we interact, the design has placed us in a very strange position vis-à-vis our emotional adaptations. Still, whatever the basis for these evident design flaws of the human mind, trigger decoding can do a great deal to overcome the problems inherent in this evolved architecture. Let's turn now to the most complete version of this process and study it with devoted care.

CHAPTER 12

Moving Toward Unconscious Meaning

The full measure of trigger decoding is a vital process, well worth mastering. But doing so requires effort because the human mind is naturally designed to resist and place obstacles against carrying out this process—it prefers to let sleeping dogs lie, even though they are dragging us along by our ears.

Fortunately, the same defensively inclined human mind is sufficiently endowed to overcome these obstacles and outwit itself. After all, we were not designed to fly, but we found ways to do it. Learning how to fully trigger decode your daydreams is far more important than flying—even to the moon. The plan here is to slowly walk through the complete process of trigger decoding your daydreams so you can make use of its rewards every day of your life.

As we saw, the adaptive sequence that we are dealing with in real life begins with the trigger event. Yet, in most instances, the decoding process begins with the daydream and its themes. We begin at the end of an adaptive process to reconstruct what happened and to discover what the final images tell us about what we experienced unconsciously and how we can best deal with the issues involved.

We have already explored what we can learn from the surface of a daydream, in light of the triggers that are known consciously to have prompted these manifest themes. We also studied the basic, simplified trigger decoding process. We now want to develop a process that will bring us the widest possible range of insights and coping strategies that the deep unconscious part of the mind can offer us.

In essence, you will be learning how to begin with a daydream and end up with extensive decoded insights and adaptive resources that were not available to you before.

Let's be very clear on this point, because it's what gives trigger decoding its power and importance: We are seeking insights and adaptive solutions that our conscious minds are entirely unaware of and unable to commandeer, even though our deep unconscious minds are quite in touch with them. This means, of course, that the best answers to your emotional dilemmas and even your emotional symptoms are right there, camouflaged in your daydreams, awaiting trigger decoding. There is no other known way to arrive at these answers.

The Eight Steps to Trigger Decoding

You can learn how the mind works by starting with a trigger event, processing the daydreams it evokes, and eventually decoding their meanings.

But, in the real world, we fail to notice and thus repress many important triggers and much of their critical meaning, so we can seldom get in touch with our unconscious minds by starting with a trigger and decoding our responsive stories.

Trigger events frighten us far more than do the encoded messages that are disguised reactions to these same events and their meanings.

This means that in searching for deep insight, it is easier to start with daydreams and their themes—and associations to their images—than it is to start with the trigger event.

This will, then, be the approach we will take to model the complete trigger decoding process. However, be clear that if you are indeed aware of a strong trigger event and some of its more compelling meanings, you actually can begin with the trigger, generate and process your daydreams, and arrive at trigger decoded insights by that route as well.

Turning now to the more usual sequence, the steps for the complete process of trigger decoding are:

Step One. Recalling one or more recent daydreams and/or creating one or more for the processing effort.

Step Two. Associating to the daydream elements, its specific details and images. As we will see, these associations should be in storied form rather than explanations or analyses of the daydream. In principle, they also should be about real events and should have power and relevance to frames and ground rules.

The surface daydream and the associations to the daydream embody a set of themes called *the daydream-associational network* or, more simply, *the daydream pool of themes, the narrative pool, or the pool of themes.*

Step Three. Identifying your own emotional issues, especially any emotionally charged conflict, symptom, decision, interpersonal issue, and so on, that currently concerns you. These issues are called *self-indicators* because they are indications of your need for insight and action, and, therefore, are vital in processing your daydreams to fulfill those needs.

Step Four. Identifying the *events, stimuli, or triggers* that have activated your emotion-processing mind and especially those emotionally charged trigger events that are likely to have been anxiety-provoking and, therefore, reworked unconsciously in your deep unconscious mind.

Step Five. Keeping the triggers in mind, extract the most compelling themes in your daydream narrative pool in order to detach these themes from the surface or manifest story. Once extracted, they can be linked to the trigger events to which they are related.

Step Six. Linking the themes to the triggers. This is done by treating the themes as encoded perceptions and adaptive recommendations in response to the trigger event. The themes reflect what you actually have experienced and how those experiences should be dealt with.

It is stressed that the themes in a narrative pool reflect actual unconscious experiences and their meanings. They are not fantasies divorced from reality, nor are they wishes and the like. They are in the main products of your imagination as it creates images that reflect the mind's reworking of real events.

Daydreams encode the actualities of a trigger event as personally and selectively perceived outside of awareness.

Step Seven: Decoding the coping strategies advocated by your deep unconscious intelligence.

Step Eight: Using your insights into your unconscious experience to explain the unconscious basis for your self-indicators.

The final two steps are the payoff for the entire process. Decoded insights related to unconscious experience pertain to triggers that are having a profound, however unconscious, effect on your emotional life. Using these insights and your own unconsciously recommended coping strategies when dealing with emotional issues affords you the best possible adaptations to your emotional impingements.

Notice that emotionally charged trigger events evoke behavioral responses, including emotional symptoms and other dysfunctions on the one hand, and, on the other, both conscious and unconscious communications—direct and encoded messages.

Both communication and behavior (broadly defined) are reactions to trigger events; they are, therefore, equivalent.

Because of this equation, trigger decoding an encoded message reveals the unconscious meanings of your dysfunctional behavioral responses—symptoms, errant actions, misguided decisions—to that same trigger. Trigger decoded insights, therefore, disclose how these unconscious experiences are affecting you and also show you how to deal with them and the emotional issues they have created.

Trigger decoded insights illuminate emotional issues, symptoms, and conflicts, and direct you to the best available solutions to your emotional dilemmas.

Summing Up

This, then, is the process you must carry out to fully trigger decode your daydreams. *The essence of the process comes down to linking your triggers to your themes; triggers and themes are at the heart of the effort.*

If we were to boil the process down to its essence, we would say:

1. Find or create a daydream.
2. Associate fresh stories to the images of the daydream.
3. Extract the main themes from the pool of themes so created.
4. Find your triggers.
5. Link the themes to the triggers, so the themes tell you how you unconsciously experienced the trigger event and what to do about it.

In substance, your working goal is to build a large and strong network of themes and then carefully pursue the identification of your active triggers until you find one that ties into your themes, to allow for their decoding in light of the meanings of the trigger experience.

Keeping trigger events separated from the themes that encode deeply unconscious perceptions of those events is our primary communicative defense. Trigger decoding undoes that defense and reduces the great cost we pay to sustain it.

Let's turn now to an illustrative vignette to help us develop a working sense of the first steps in this vital process.

Initiating the Decoding Process

Ben, a single man in his early 30s, has a daydream image of lying on a beach in Puerto Rico. An attractive blonde woman comes over to him and asks if she can buy him a drink.

Abruptly, he breaks off his daydream—it's too good to be true, he thinks.

Question 12.1

What kind of daydream is this? Looking over its surface images, what can you say about it—and about Ben? We know nothing about the triggers for the daydream, but can you suggest two trigger events that could have prompted its imagery? Explain the basis for your answer.

Answer 12.1

This is a denial/escapist daydream with two very positive elements. In itself, it tells us little about Ben or daydreaming. We could say Ben is in a state of wish fulfillment. However, based on our study of escapist daydreams, we could also speculate that Ben may be trying to deny or escape from a major trauma of some kind. Still, a brief daydream of this kind need not necessarily imply the denial of a major issue—we have enough minor traumas to cope with each day, so we're entitled to our allotment of happy daydreams. We need to know more to be able to say more about Ben and his daydream.

As for triggers, there are two kinds of possibilities. The first would speak for any conceivable trauma the daydream could be running away from. The second would involve something already encoded in the imagery because escapist daydreams are products of the unconscious creative center that encodes daydream imagery, which means, of course, that they are vehicles of unconscious perceptions and their processing, as well as a means of flight.

As long as we take an escapist daydream at face value, we have no way of appreciating the intricacies of its structure. As a rule, to delve into and benefit from its deeper, disguised meanings, we need to associate to the elements of the daydream and allow them to bring forth additional narrative material. Indeed, as we will soon see, the processing of any daydream actually requires that we associate to its images.

Associating to the elements of a daydream can vastly enrich the network of themes available for linking them to trigger events.

Associating to Daydream Elements

This brings us to the vital need to learn how to associate to daydream elements. It also will serve us well to appreciate why associating plays such a great role in enabling us to realize the full promise of our daydream experiences.

In principle:

1.   Processing a daydream should always include *associating to its main elements*—the people, settings, and events of the daydream story.

2.   This associational effort is called *guided associating.* This method replaces the free associating connected with psychoanalysis that has characterized the way many people work with their dreams. In free associating to a daydream, the daydreamer is free to let his or her mind wander wherever it wishes to go—which often is quite far from the daydream images. The result generally is a weak collection of associations, many of them intellectual musings with virtually no encoded qualities—the very attribute you're trying to promote.

All in all, free associating does not facilitate the development of a powerful or especially meaningful pool of themes.

In guided associating, however, the daydreamer is constrained by a requirement that he or she *concentrate on associating to the individ-*

ual elements of a daydream, with the associations being in narrative/storied form. The daydreamer is asked to return again and again to the details of the daydream story to bring to mind fresh stories and images.

By this means, the power and meaning of the generated pool of themes is greatly enhanced.

While momentary lapses are inevitable, guided associating usually produces a strong and full pool of narrative themes that is ideal for linking triggers to produce deep unconscious insight.

3.   In almost all cases, the associations to a daydream are more powerful and cogent than the images in the manifest daydream itself.

It can truly be said that daydreams are imagined to be associated to rather than analyzed.

4.   As noted, daydreams are developed by an unconscious creative center that operates through condensation. This means that each detail in a daydream story has packed into its configuration two or more additional stories. Each element of a daydream is a marker for several stories, and these stories materialize when we associate to the daydream images.

5.   From this, it follows that the key to associating to a daydream is to be sure you:

> *a.* Associate to as many of the details of a daydream as possible.
> *b.* Generate associations that are stories instead of intellectualizations and explanations which have virtually no encoded qualities.
> *c.* Go back to each detail of a daydream several times, ensuring that fresh stories come to mind each time.

6.   The ideal associated story has power, is often frame-related, and involves *a shift away from the scene of the surface daydream into other times, places, and people.*

7. The more diverse your stories, the more useful your pool of themes for trigger decoding—you want variety more than repetition in your narratives and their themes.

8. *These associated stories should be as specific and detailed as possible.* Often, a person or a place or a time period will come to mind first; if so, it is critical to pursue the image until you get to a specific event and tell that story.

Let's go back to Ben. Having stopped imaging, he turns to guided associating to his two daydream elements. His first thought is that he'd love to be in Puerto Rico at this very moment because he has so many business problems these days. Puerto Rico is a lovely island and he certainly likes the warm climate.

Self-observation

Let's pause here to establish another critical feature of processing our daydreams. An important facet of the productive processing of a daydream is the use of *self-observation*—the quiet, continual, conscious monitoring of the trigger decoding effort. To do this effectively, *you need a clear model of the process* so you can decide if you are on or off track. If you notice that you've wandered away from the process—not an uncommon occurrence—you can put yourself back on track.

> *Indeed, because you are running counter to the design of the mind that prevents you from consciously accessing your deep unconscious experience, you will, in processing a daydream, inevitably stray from the process from time to time. Monitoring the effort is the only means by which you can ensure seeing the processing through to a successful end.*

To list the elements is an essential guideline to the process, the path from the surface daydream to its encoded secrets is:

1. Begin with a daydream story.
2. Engage in narrative guided associating.
3. Continue with element number two above until you have sufficient power and frame-related imagery.
4. Extract the main themes from the daydream narrative pool.
5. Identify your most compelling trigger events and select them one at a time for linking.
6. Link the extracted themes to the triggers, yielding trigger decoded insights.

Question 12.2

Look at Ben's initial thoughts after his daydream was finished. Are they guided associations? Do they comply with the rules of guided associating? Explain the basis for your answer.

Answer 12.2

These thoughts are indeed guided associations, but they are intellectual in nature. They are not stories.

The invocation of intellectual thoughts is typical of our initial and later responses to daydream imagery. It is a way of avoiding the narratives that carry encoded meaning. If Ben fails to realize he is intellectualizing, he is likely to continue doing so for quite a while. On the other hand, if he catches what he's doing, he can get back on course by immediately switching to storied guided associations.

The path from a manifest daydream to a deeply unconscious insight is a very narrow one and is easily left. Stepping back from time to time while processing a daydream to see where you are is absolutely essential to keeping yourself on the path as much as possible.

Narrative Guided Associations

Ben realizes he's not narrating. He shifts his mode of thinking and recalls an incident a year earlier in which he was in Jamaica and a man was robbed on his hotel's beach. The robber posed as a member of the hotel staff and took the man's wallet. At that time, Ben was there with his girlfriend Kitty, which reminded him that Kitty had had her purse stolen at the airport before they left on their trip together. Kitty had wanted to marry Ben but he didn't feel ready for that kind of commitment, so they had stopped seeing each other soon after that trip.

Jamaica also brings to mind another love affair Ben had two years earlier with a woman named Cass. He had gone to Europe with Cass and together they had sunned on the beaches of the Riviera. But it had been a stormy trip, largely because they had quarreled over Cass' involvement with another man. Also, a man at their hotel was found murdered. It was suspected that drug dealing was involved.

The blonde woman brings to mind Grace, a woman who is dating Ben's friend Al. Grace has strong business connections and helped Ben land a very lucrative business contract. She also has a brother with cerebral palsy. Grace's parents recently had manipulated her brother into receiving care at a clinic at which he was ineligible to be seen.

Question 12.3

Are these narrative guided associations? Even now, before we study these issues, can you detect any powerful or frame-related themes? Explain the basis for your answers.

Answer 12.3

These are indeed detailed, narrative guided associations, with both power (e.g., theft, murder, illness) and frame allusions (e.g., again, theft and murder, which violate the law, but also marriage and getting the ill brother into a facility where he did not belong). On the manifest level, this daydream has little direct or encoded meaning, yet as a source of guided associations, it proved capable of generating a notably complex and strong pool of themes.

This is an excellent illustration of why associating to daydream elements is such an important part of processing a daydream—it is the major source of power and meaning for a narrative pool of themes.

Question 12.4

Use the themes of Ben's daydream narrative pool to suggest at least two possible trigger events that could have prompted his imagery.

Answer 12.4

Because the daydream is escapist in nature, and in light of the powerful themes in Ben's guided associations, we have reasons to suspect that a strongly traumatic trigger event had indeed set his imagination in motion. If we recall that the nature of the imagery has been shaped by the nature of the trigger event that evoked it, we could propose that the trigger might involve an issue between Ben and a girlfriend, and that something terrible or violent had transpired, despite her having been helpful to Ben in some significant way. Thus, the trigger could be that someone had stolen Ben's girlfriend from him, or that his life could be in jeopardy.

The actual trigger event was that Ben's present girlfriend, to whom he was engaged, suddenly ran off with Ben's best friend. The friend had not only stolen her from Ben, but had destroyed an important relationship and a piece of Ben in so doing. The image of murder encoded not only Ben's unconscious experience of the incident, but also his own murderous rage against his fiance and friend.

Beneath our happy daydreams lies much unhappiness. The issues are usually heavily encoded into the positive surface imagery and can be brought to light only through guided associating. But before we deal further with the properties and functions of guided associations, let's close this chapter with an exercise.

Exercise 12.1

Take one of your spontaneous daydreams or invent a daydream for this exercise. Try your hand at guided associating. First, let your mind go wherever it wishes. In time, observe what you have done— were you engaged in guided or free associating, or both? Were you telling specific stories or general ones, or none at all because you were explaining, interpreting, and intellectualizing? Now associate some fresh stories to the elements of your daydream. In addition, as best you can, make sure there are some powerful images in these associated stories.

Comment 12.1

Most people find that their mind tends to intellectualize when associating to daydreams. They elaborate on the details of their initial daydream images, explain and interpret what they mean, or offer general impressions of the daydream story. It requires astute efforts of self-observation to detect these trends and modify them so you shift to guided associating with much-needed storied images.

Once you begin to develop narrative guided associations, the tendency is to tell general stories or to allude to repetitive incidents without recounting a specific tale. In these instances, the strategy is to take all such allusions as markers and *go from the general to the specific—* for example, from a time period in your life to a specific event from that era.

The deep unconscious mind expresses itself through very specific and detailed narratives; anything short of that is defensive and incomplete.

These compromised ways of dealing with daydream images reflect the defensive posture of the conscious mind in respect to encoded, unconscious communications. Learning and enforcing the proper way to associate to daydream elements takes you a long way toward countering these communicative defenses. Processing your daydreams toward specific insights requires determination, concentration, effective self-observation, and a dogged insistence on pursuing this gift-giving process.

CHAPTER 13

Power and Frames

The deep unconscious system of the emotion processing mind deals exclusively with compelling and potentially disruptive, anxiety-provoking trigger events and meanings. These issues are definitively communicated through *power themes*—contents that reflect critical areas of experience and conflict for all humans. If you are going to access the workings of this deep system, you are obligated to generate daydream networks with powerful themes. The absence of these themes means you are not negotiating the world of deep unconscious experience. In this context, it's well to be reminded that guided associating is your greatest resource in this regard.

With only rare exceptions, the stories generated in guided associating to daydream elements have more power than the daydream itself.

Power Themes

In defining the power of your daydream imagery, be clear that power themes *appear on the surface of a daydream or in guided associations to its images*—they are quite manifest. They are not brought to bear via implication or interpretation, but are openly alluded to in the direct imagery. A sexual theme is openly sexual in the daydream, a violent theme openly violent. It is not a matter of believing someone is behaving in a seductive way—either there is a seduction going on in the daydream story or the theme is not present.

The use of these themes to reveal *unconscious meaning* does not depend on fathoming the implications of a set of themes—implications belong to the surface of the daydream and the conscious system. Instead, the themes are used as stated and *the unconscious component is revealed entirely through the connection or link to the trigger event.*

> *The encoded themes, then, are stated as such; they appear manifestly in a daydream or the associations to its elements. Their encoding function is disclosed through the discovery that a theme developed in the context of one story has a meaning in the context of another story—that of the trigger event.*

Aside from frame-related themes (see below), there are only three classes of power themes:

1. *Manifest themes of sexuality.* Sexual themes are powerful because sexual issues are a universal source of conflict. More important, *many nonsexual emotionally charged trigger events have a latent or unconsciously sexual quality and meaning.* While manifestly and consciously, these triggers, which usually involve violations of ground rules and frames, do not entail overt sexual experiences, they do have an inherent unconscious sexual charge. This realization is important in two ways: first, we need to know that nonsexual triggers can activate *unconscious sexualized perceptions and conflicts,* and second, that the effects that these triggers have on us are definitively colored by these unconscious sexual qualities.

> *It is stressed that the unconscious experience of sexual qualities to frame modifying trigger events is not a distortion or misperception—it is a valid reading of one set of the actual unconscious meanings of the trigger event.*

As noted, the most common type of nonsexual trigger event that is fraught with unconscious sexual meanings is modification or violation of rules, laws, boundaries, and frames. The deep unconscious system is exceedingly sensitive to frame-related actions and they are a large but unappreciated part of our everyday lives. Their unconscious sexual meanings—for example, sexual assault, seductions, forced sexual satisfactions, etc.—have a profound unconscious effect on the reactions we have to frame breakers and, via displacement, to other people in our lives.

2. *Themes of death, harm, damage, and illness.* This group of harmful themes—*the damage package*—includes all forms of physical threat and harm. Specific themes include death, illness, assault and attack, physical disabilities, loss of limbs, loss of people, and the like. As a group, they engender issues of death anxiety as part of their meanings. Violence, illness, loss, and death-related problems are inherently anxiety-provoking and, therefore, constitute a powerful set of themes. But here, too, these qualities also are inherent to non-violent frame modifications in that types of rule-breaking express violence and cause harm to self and others.

3. *Images that are unlikely in reality.* Strange and unrealistic images are not uncommon in daydreams. They do not imply mental illness or madness. They do, however, speak for very powerful trigger events, often with inherently contradictory messages that drive people crazy. It is crucial to associate to these kinds of images when they appear in a surface daydream. Yet, because of their links to powerful and maddening issues, they often prove difficult to associate to—which is all the more reason to press for storied associations to these elements.

These, then, are the themes that speak for a powerful pool of daydream themes. Without such allusions, there is little chance of attaining compelling insights even if the key trigger event is known. With them, however, there's a promise of deep understanding and the process moves to the search for trigger events and linking triggers to themes.

Rules, Laws, and Boundaries—Frames

As I said, the other area of great concern to the deep unconscious system of the emotion-processing mind is the issue of rules and boundaries—frames. In general, the conscious mind pays only minimal attention to ground rule and frame-related experiences. And, in general, the inclinations of this system of the mind lean toward frame modifications rather than adherence to rules and boundaries—consciously, we are all inclined to some degree to sanction and favor rule-breaking.

In contrast, the deep unconscious system is both exceedingly frame sensitive as reflected in its encoded messages, and the system consistently advocates adhering to or securing rather than modifying frames. For the deep unconscious mind, frame-related behaviors are central to its view of the world and because of this sensitivity, frame impingements have strong effects on our experience of others (and ourselves). The state of a frame determines the kinds of meaning we ascribe to the actions and words of others, and how we react to them. As a result of this focus, frame allusions in our daydreams are exceedingly common and have special importance.

The emergence of frame-related themes in a network of daydream images speaks for the active presence of a frame-related trigger event. The event may go in one of two directions—there are two kinds of fundamental frames—*secured-constricting frames and altered, modified or deviant frames*. The frame-related imagery in a daydream thus can be either *frame-securing or frame-modifying*. The type of imagery indicates the kind of frame-related trigger event with which that daydreamer is dealing.

In general, the ultimate decision as to whether a particular action is frame-securing or frame-deviant is determined by the deep unconscious system's encoded responses to the frame impingement. This in turn, reflected in the disguised imagery of the daydream network that has been evoked by the frame-related behavior in question. Positive, affirming, safety-related, supportive imagery speaks for a securing of or adherence to the ideal frame, while negative, destructive, persecutory, and unsafe imagery bears testimony to frame alterations.

When frames are maintained and secured, there is an experience of enormous support and security, but there also is a deep, secured frame anxiety that is aroused by the constricting, limiting, and entrapping qualities of every secured frame moment. After all, adhering to a ground rule limits your unbridled freedom and implies acceptance of limits and constraints. There also is a link between the entrapping qualities of the secured frame and the experience of personal death—we are all born into a claustrum or closed space from which there is no escape except through death.

Secured frames are the ultimate context of support and yet a source of unbearable, usually unconscious, death-related anxieties.

On the other hand, violations or modifications of ground rules and boundaries provide temporary relief from these feelings of limitation and entrapment. But frame deviations also persecute and harm others—and ultimately yourself.

The deviant frame offers immediate relief, but does so at great cost to self and others.

Secured and Altered Frames

To clarify this critical dimension that is so familiar to your unconscious mind, yet so unfamiliar to your conscious mind, let's develop a few perspectives. Every relationship and every situation in your life has a setting and a context, a stage on which your interactions unfold. The context includes:

1. The physical setting and the background nature of the basic relationship that you have with the people with whom you're interacting.
2. The physical and psychological boundaries between yourself and them.
3. A body of background social-cultural rules, mores, laws, regulations, and the like.

The physical part of our frames or frameworks creates the actual setting and physical boundaries for our interactions. This includes locales, buildings, rooms, vehicles, and so on. The secured or ideal frame is constituted by a safe and secure physical setting, as when a child lives in a home or apartment and has his or her own room to sleep in, an employee has a private office, or a teacher has a closed-door classroom. Changes in locales, the absence of a secured space, and damage to physical boundaries like walls are common types of frame breaks.

The psychological aspects of frames include all levels of rules and law—international, national, and local—as well as family and other social guidelines. These ground rules define and regulate our relationships and interactions.

There is, as I said, an ideal set of ground rules that support and protect us and allow us to grow, flourish, and function well. The model of the ideal frame exists in the deep unconscious system of every mind—there is indeed a universal secured frame, at least for Western cultures. Undoubtedly, the model is created in each of us through the unconscious experience of frame-related impingements (securing or deviating) that occur from infancy on.

Each major life situation has its setting and context, and a set of explicitly and implicitly defined rules—family, school, love, work, friendships, and such. Adhering to these rules creates the backdrop for one kind of relationship, while modifying these unconsciously defined rules creates quite a different situation.

Secured frames enhance our functioning and foster trust, a sense of safety and security, creativity and growth, but they also generate a measure of secured frame, entrapment anxiety—a type of silent anxiety that is linked to death anxiety. These anxieties are very intense, although usually quite unconscious. Secured frames provide us with the best possible conditions for relating and living, but generate extremes of anxiety that compel us unwittingly to modify frames of all kinds—a common occurrence in today's world.

Altered frames provide us with some temporary relief from entrapment, death-related, and other kinds of anxieties, but they always are damaging, persecutory, harmful to self and others, and, on some level, they disturb our relationships and functioning. However, our feelings of helplessness in the face of death and death–related traumas unconsciously motivate each of us to seek out a measure of modified frame. We break many frames, large and small, and back up these ultimately hurtful behaviors with considerable denial of the ultimate cost in pain, suffering and loss of creativity that we pay for these transgressions.

Exercise 13.1

Recall your daydreams from the past 24 hours. With utmost spontancity, make up at least two additional daydreams. Associate to as many of the daydream elements as you can. Now harvest the imagery and identify all the frame-related themes you can find. Notice if they are frame-securing or frame–modifying. Next, turn to your past 24 hours and list all of the actual frame–related incidents and behaviors—yours and others—that you can recall. Again, decide if these incidents were frame–securing or frame–modifying. Overall, get a sense of how often frame allusions and impingements appear in your daydream imagery and in your real life.

Comment 13.1

You will likely be quite surprised to see how many daydream images and how many real events touch on frame–related themes. They are extremely common even though the conscious mind tends to pay little attention to them. Frame modifications— the preference of the conscious system—almost always are more common than frame–securing efforts.

If you are able to trigger decode your stories in response to a recent frame–deviant trigger event, you are certain to discover for yourself that the deep unconscious mind is exceedingly frame–sensitive and consistently advocates adherence to the secured frame, through its encoded daydream narratives. Here too, the deep unconscious mind seems the wiser: Boundary and frame conditions are critical to the functioning and very existence of all living and nonliving systems and entities—the cell and the human body being prime examples of this principle.

The deep unconscious mind speaks a language that is built around frame impingements, the hub around which everything else revolves.

Guided Associating in Action

Let's take an extended look at a daydream experience to integrate and illustrate the main principles we have developed regarding guided associating.

Wendy is a single woman in her late 20s. She's home one evening and has a daydream that begins with her sitting in a coffee bar drinking espresso and eating a piece of cake. A woman enters the coffee bar. Although Wendy doesn't know her, the woman sits down at Wendy's table and takes a piece of Wendy's cake and eats it. A man joins them and Wendy stands up and screams at them to go away. She takes her coffee cup and moves to another table, leaving the cake behind. The man and woman follow Wendy to the new table, so she gets up and runs out of the coffee bar. After a while, she looks back and the woman and man are gone. She realizes she's in a lovely neighborhood, bathed in a warm summer morning sun.

Question 13.1

To begin at the beginning, what type of daydream is this? Looking at the isolated daydream, what can you say about its imagery and its creator, Wendy? Given that it has themes, suggest two trigger events that could have prompted the daydream imagery.

Answer 13.1

An isolated daydream is a bare–boned set of images. We could speculate that Wendy is trying to find peace and satisfaction, and that something is interfering with her pursuit of those goals. She seems to feel intruded upon by at least two people and seems to be helpless to deal with them except by flight. Escape evidently leads to tranquility. And if you want to use psychoanalyticese, you could propose that Wendy seems to have an oral fixation, severe conflicts with women, and oedipal issues as well. However, be wary of such formulations because they do little more than translate imagery into intellectual jargon.

As you can see, in the absence of known triggers, the formulations you can offer simply reiterate the manifest themes of the daydream and treat them as concerns and threats that Wendy seems to be experiencing. We need to know more about Wendy and a lot more about her specific triggers to say anything that smacks of surprise and deeper meaning.

As for possible triggers for this daydream, they're likely to involve an intrusion by an unwelcome person or two, an incident in which something has been taken or stolen from Wendy, something that interrupted her solitude, or something that had been invasive in some way. To sample some specific possibilities, Wendy might have been forced to share a room with someone, someone may have stolen her purse, her parents might have come unannounced into the bathroom while she was taking a bath, or a boyfriend might have asked Wendy to become involved in a ménage à trois. These triggers fit the themes of this story like a glove fits a hand.

A daydream belongs to the daydreamer. So, before we get to Wendy's guided associations and triggers, let's learn a little more about her. Wendy lives at home with her parents and works as an administrator for a hospital. She's been dating a young man named Walter for two years and he wants to get married. For reasons she can't quite articulate, Wendy is reluctant to do so and has not accepted his standing proposal of marriage. At work, she gets along well with most of her fellow workers, but she has felt some unpleasant vibes from her immediate boss Aaron, who often says strange things to her, though here, too, Wendy can't quite say what's strange about them.

Adding Fresh Stories

Wendy rethinks her story and begins her guided associating. The woman reminds her of Walter's mother, who seems to have too much power over her son. Walter lives in his own apartment, and Wendy remembers an incident when his mother showed up there unannounced while she and Walter were making love in his bedroom. Wendy felt violated, embarrassed, and enraged. Walter's mother still cooks for her son and brings him food packages; he should cut loose from her, Wendy feels.

The coffee bar is in a neighborhood that Wendy likes a lot. She often meets two of her girlfriends, Sylvia and Alicia, there; they live together and have a lovely apartment. It's a nice arrangement, but there had been a problem—Alicia's mother had taken an overdose of sleeping pills when her daughter went off to live on her own. Now that Wendy thinks about it, the man and woman actually looked like Alicia's parents whom Wendy had met when their daughter had gotten engaged some time back. Her fiance turned out to be a philanderer who had several other girlfriends despite his engagement; Alicia eventually gave him back his ring and stopped seeing him. She's been dating someone much nicer ever since.

The two people eating her cake brought to mind Wendy's sister Della, who works as a hostess in a restaurant known for their dessert pastries. Before Della left home she took—actually, stole—several of Wendy's outfits. Wendy had tried to get them back, but Della hid them in a closet and claimed she hadn't taken them; eventually, Wendy gave up the chase.

Wendy next recalls a time when Della broke her leg skiing. Their mother was vindictive because she objected to her daughter's involvement in what she called a high-risk, unnecessary sport. Wendy's sister had a weird feeling that someone had pushed her down while she was skiing, but no one was nearby. Nevertheless, she was convinced that the ghost of a friend who had recently died had done it.

Finally, Wendy associates to another incident in which Della went on a business trip and was trapped in an elevator with a man with whom she worked. At first, Della panicked and was fearful that the man would abuse her, but he proved to be very reassuring and she calmed down until they were rescued. The experience actually brought Della and the man closer to each other and they became involved in an affair, which lasted about a year, until he got involved with another woman.

There were other guided associations to this daydream, but we have a lot to work with already. Wendy has generated some strong and varied, narrative guided associations to her daydream elements. This is a good illustration of this part of the decoding process.

Back to the Frame

To develop the frame allusions in Wendy's network of themes, I will first ask a question.

Question 13.2

Think about Wendy's daydream and her associations to its images. List all of the frame allusions you can identify. For each one, indicate whether it is frame-secured or frame-modified in nature.

Answer 13.2

The original daydream has frame allusions to the coffee bar, a physical setting which is secure at first, but then invaded by the man and woman who then modify that frame. The couple that eats Wendy's cake is a frame break—an incursion into her interpersonal boundaries and a violation of the law. The lovely neighborhood is a positive and secured setting.

In the associations, Walter has his own apartment, which is a secured setting. He and Wendy are making love in his bedroom, which is secure, but then his mother enters the apartment unannounced—she invades the space and violates its security, and intrudes upon the interpersonal boundaries of both Walter and Wendy. The mother's over-involvement with her son also modifies the acceptable interpersonal boundaries between her and Walter.

In the next association, there is a nice, holding neighborhood and the shared apartment, which is a partly secured but nevertheless modified setting—sharing the apartment is a departure from the ideal frame of having one's own space. Attempting suicide departs from some moral codes and, in some places, it is a violation of the law; it also is an attempt to modify the boundary line between life and death so that death occurs.

Alicia's philandering fiance is a frame breaker. His engagement to her secured a relationship frame and, of course, Alicia's breaking the engagement modified the frame of the relationship with her fiance, but secured Alicia's personal relationship frame—she disengaged herself from a frame-breaking fiance. Frame issues abound in that situation.

The restaurant is the sister's work frame. Her stealing Wendy's dresses is, of course, a frame violation, and hiding them in a closet alludes to a physical frame. The sister's entrapment in the elevator speaks for secured frame, entrapment anxieties—the positive side is reflected in the image of the reassuring friend, while the anxious side is seen in the sister's panic over being trapped in the elevator, and her fears of abuse. The affair with a co-worker modifies the ideal frame where social and business relationships are kept separate, and the break-up of the affair oddly enough secures that frame modification—despite the sense of loss.

We have generated a long list of frame images without knowledge of their triggering events. Every one of these frame-related images has been evoked by a frame-related action on Wendy's part or on the part of someone else who interacted with her. But I've taken the liberty of omitting the adaptive side of Wendy's life in order to help you get acquainted with frame-related themes and their abundance—and just how unnoticed they tend to be.

Keep in mind that:

1. Rules and boundaries—frames—are the single most neglected aspect of human experience.
2. For your deep unconscious mind and for you as a total person, frame-related events and behaviors are among the most critical trigger events with which you cope every day of your life—most of it quite unconsciously.

3. Secured-frame anxiety, which is a powerful form of death anxiety, is among the most important unrecognized aspect of human dread.

4. In terms of daydream imagery, a true secured-frame moment will produce two kinds of themes—those that are very positive and reflect of health-giving aspects of that type of frame, and entrapment imagery, that reflects the secured-frame anxieties evoked by the frame-securing action.

Back to Power

Let's turn now to the issue of power themes.

Question 13.3

Review Wendy's daydream and her associations, and identify all of the power themes you can find.

Answer 13.3

In characteristic fashion, the original daydream has little power. The one possible, rather weak, power image is the couple that eat sWendy's cake, which, in addition to its frame deviant quality, also is somewhat assaultive.

The associations do, however, bring with them a greater measure of power, such as Wendy's having sex with Walter and then Alicia's mother's suicide attempt, a notable form of self-directed violence and an allusion to the possibility of death. Then, too, there are the sister's stealing Wendy's clothes and lying about not having them, as well as her having an accident, breaking her leg, and believing that she had been pushed by a ghost—an image unlikely in reality. Other power themes include the betrayal of Alicia's fiance, the affair of Wendy's sister, and the loss of that boyfriend.

All in all, the daydream network contains manifest power themes related to each of the categories of power—sexuality, the damage group, and unreal events. Quite typically, the associated stories have considerably more power than the original, surface daydream. Because the deep unconscious system deals only with powerful perceptions and issues, you can see why it's essential to associate to your daydreams. There is no better way of building a workable pool of themes.

We have a thematic pool with both frame-related and powerful themes. We therefore are ready to move on and carry out the next steps in processing this daydream. We're heading toward linking these themes with their triggers, so clearly we need the trigger events that prompted these images. You may have already used the themes in Wendy's narrative pool to get a line on their triggers. After all:

Whenever you're working with daydream themes, you should be thinking and wondering about their trigger events — triggers and themes are the keys to the unconscious mind.

It's time, then, to examine Wendy's triggers—and to learn how, in principle, to deal with trigger events in processing a daydream.

CHAPTER 14

Getting to Triggers

There are two sides to processing daydreams. On one side are the narratives and their themes, *the encoded messages*. On the other side are *the triggers, the events to which the themes are a coping response.* The goal of trigger decoding is to bring these two sides together to produce decoded insights.

Trigger events are emotionally charged incidents that impact the emotion-processing mind. Triggers are traumas, helpful moments, hurts, illnesses, deaths, and anything else with a notable emotional impact on the human psyche.

The Two Effects of Triggers

These events have two effects on us, both mediated through conscious and unconscious processing and adaptations. The first is *communicative,* in that triggers evoke manifest and encoded narrative messages. This communicative response enables us to get a line on the conscious and unconscious meanings the trigger event has had. Understanding meaning enables us to comprehend the issues that the trigger experience has created for us and to better shape our adaptive responses to the event.

The communicative part of the responses to trigger events is, of course, where trigger decoding plays a critical role. Understanding our unconscious responses to emotionally charged trigger events provides us with remarkably sound answers to the issues raised by these events—answers that would not otherwise be available.

The second group of responses to trigger events has a more immediate effect on the course of our lives.

Triggers evoke emotional, bodily, and behavioral responses. While meaningful communicative responses to trigger events allow for thought and planned coping, especially after trigger decoding has been achieved, behavioral responses are another matter. This latter group of reactions to triggers, while also meaningful, is too ill-defined to decode. Nevertheless, the actions we take in response to trigger events are fateful.

We react to triggers with feelings that affect our mood and, in turn, our minds and bodies—with somatic responses that can involve a wide range of physical symptoms, some of them quite serious—and with actions that, being unconsciously driven and consciously uninformed by insight, often have harmful effects on ourselves and others.

I call this second group of responses to triggers *personal woes or self-indicators* because they show how our triggers are affecting us and our lives. In response to favorable trigger events, they may be all to the good, but more often they are emotional problems that are being driven largely by traumatic trigger events and our unconscious experiences of these hurtful impingements.

To resolve these trigger-driven problems, we need to trigger decode the communicative responses to the very same triggers so we can use trigger decoded insights to resolve the difficulties.

The Goals of Trigger Decoding

The goals of trigger decoding can be stated as follows:

1.   Identifying the emotionally charged experiences that are disturbing our emotional equilibrium—trigger identification—and then illuminating the unconscious reasons why this is happening.

This goal combines trigger identification—an awareness of what's upsetting us—with trigger decoding the disguised response to the trigger.

Finding the trigger event is the key issue, and understanding what the event means to you and how it is affecting your life comes next.

2. *Illuminating the triggers and unconscious experiences that account for our self-indicators*—that is, for our emotional malfunctions and conflicts. This goal arises when a trigger event causes both a communicative response and a symptomatic behavioral response—something inadvertent that we do, a bout of anxiety or depression, a phobic symptom, an inability to work, etc. It also is a factor when we are in the throes of an emotional conflict.

This second goal is prominent in psychotherapy, the treatment of emotional symptoms. But it arises often enough in everyday life—who among us hasn't suffered a mood disturbance, a psychological symptom, or done something we think was off-base and an unneeded source of harm to ourselves and/or others? Beyond these emotional disturbances of which we are aware, there is an endless stream of actual malfunctions that we ignore, deny, or explain away—they, too, are in need of trigger decoded insights.

In these situations, the goal of trigger decoding is to link triggers to their themes as a way of illuminating the hidden, unconscious basis of our self-indicators.

This goal involves using trigger decoding to reveal the unconscious factors in our emotional difficulties and illuminate the unconscious aspects of our life decisions. Indeed, the communicative and behavioral responses to trigger events are two sides of the same attempt to cope with and adapt to an emotionally charged triggering experience—one through telling stories like daydreams, the other through a behavioral response that is an actuality of our lives.

In all, then, the same trigger event simultaneously creates our emotional problems and evokes deep unconscious processing that reveals the unconscious sources of our difficulties through encoded themes, thereby marking the path for their resolution. Such is the inventiveness of the human mind.

The main problem is that the emotional disturbance usually is blatant, while the cure is encoded—ergo, trigger decoding.

Identifying Your Critical Triggers

In processing daydreams, the greatest need and effort involves understanding your *unconscious* reactions to critical emotionally charged trigger events. Life is filled with strong triggering experiences, and every such experience is overflowing with meaning and impact. Indeed, the enormous complexities of everyday life appear to have created the social pressures that played a significant role in the evolution of the two-system mind—no single system could handle everything we must cope with each day and allow us to function well and survive. The deep unconscious system was designed to handle the over-abundance of disturbing meanings with which the conscious system could not deal ,with, much of it involving anxiety-provoking emotional stimuli in the form of events overloaded with psychological meanings.

There are many important ramifications to the finding that the human mind takes in or receives a large part of the most disturbing aspects of our triggering experiences through subliminal (unconscious), rather than conscious, perception.

For one, it means that many triggers and/or their most critical meanings for our lives are experienced outside of awareness—they are repressed. We barely, if at all, realize they exist and are affecting us.

This realization implies that we live with and respond to the most powerful events in our lives without knowing much of what we are reacting to—unless you engage in trigger decoding.

While you might imagine that it's easy to go over each day and select the most emotionally powerful events of the day, it turns out that it actually is extremely difficult to do. Remember, the human mind is designed to bar potentially disturbing emotional experiences (inputs) from awareness—that is, to not process our significant trigger events consciously. As you will discover when you engage in processing your daydreams for a while, identifying the critical triggers in your life and their most compelling meanings is a task carried out in the face of great reluctance and resistance.

Trigger searching is a hunter's mission and the prey—your triggers—are incredibly elusive.

Repressing/Forgetting Your Triggers

Repressing or forgetting significant trigger events can take any of the following forms:

1. *Forgetting entirely a traumatic event of which you had previously been aware.* This happens quite naturally each day, but will be especially strong when you sit down to trigger decode a daydream. Quite often, the highly disturbing trigger you were preoccupied with all day will now be lost to your conscious awareness. If so, the chase is on (see below).

2. *Having no conscious awareness that a given event known to you actually was a disturbing trigger.* Here, repression is activated at the very moment of the hurtful event. While you realize that something just happened, you fail to appreciate that it has had a strong emotional impact on you. The conscious mind consistently underestimates the trauma value of the things that happen to us—our triggers.

3. *Maintaining an awareness of the trigger event, but not being aware of the particular emotionally charged meanings it has had for you.* In this case, you realize an event has been traumatic, but you miss some of the most significant meanings it

has had for you. In this form, repression and denial are directed primarily at the *meanings* of the triggering event and less so at the event itself.

The human emotion-processing mind has paid an enormous price for its evolved defensiveness and self-protection. We are not inherently aware of the design flaws and processing problems of our minds; they emerge only when we adopt a definitive adaptive approach to our emotional lives. It is well to realize, then, that the massive use of repression (and denial) by the conscious mind means that:

1. You have only limited if any awareness of the fullness of the emotional traumas that are deeply affecting your life.
2. If you want to be master of your own psyche and life, you must trigger decode your daydreams routinely each day.
3. In processing your daydreams, inevitably you will encounter difficulties identifying your most significant trigger events. You will need to work hard to capture your key triggers and the unconscious meanings that they had and have for you—the meanings that your deep unconscious system has processed unconsciously and encoded into your daydreams.

Exercise 14.1

Before we discuss the best ways to discover your significant triggers, perform this exercise. This evening, sit or lie down in a comfortable place where you can be alone for a while; then list in your mind the most important trigger events from earlier in your day. That done, turn to your daydreams, make up two stories on the spot and associate to their elements. Using the thematic pool you have created, try to develop a sense of the triggers to which they could be linked. Now list your triggers again, adding anything that you had missed that now seems important. Indicate the triggers that seem to you traumatic—and the meanings to which you are reacting. Compare your first and second trigger lists—which seems most complete and on the mark?

Comment 14.1

Most people will find that their initial trigger list turns out, in light of a second try, to be incomplete in important ways. You also may have the experience of completing this exercise and then, while falling asleep or at some other moment, suddenly thinking of an important trigger you left off your list.

With these problems in mind, let's look now at the strategies that can help you discover most or even all of the significant triggers you are dealing with each day.

Two Types of Trigger Searches

There are two methods you can use to ferret out your trigger events and their key unconscious meanings. They are:

1. *The direct search for trigger events.* Once you have finished associating to a daydream, the next step is, of course, embarking on a search for your active triggers. These are the initial measures you should use:

 a. Make a direct effort to consciously review your day and look for the significant events that took place.

 b. As you do this, generate a *mental list* of your significant triggers. Make the list as complete as possible.

 c. Once this list seems complete for the moment, place the triggers on your list in order, positioning the most compelling and traumatic triggers at the top of the list. Special emphasis should be given to death-related incidents and issues, and to frame-related impingements—frame-modifying or frame-securing.

Examples of the frame-modifying group of triggers are the loss of a job, the death of someone, an inappropriate seduction, stealing, and the like. Illustrative of the frame-securing group of triggers are deciding to stay with a job, getting married, starting classes at a new school, and so on. The possible strings of important triggers in our day-to-day lives is virtually infinite. You want your list to be complete because when you get to the next step in the process—linking your triggers to the encoded themes—you will work your way from the most compelling triggers down to those that are notable but least important.

Once you have your list of significant triggers, you can either move on to the linking process or turn to the second method of searching for triggers in an effort to ensure as complete a list as possible. In general, memory-based trigger lists tend to be incomplete—they are strongly affected by the defensive and repressive needs of the conscious mind. Making these lists is, however, aided by your developing a body of knowledge about human nature in general and your own sensitivities in particular—that is, knowing what sets you off emotionally. At some point in processing a daydream, then, you should routinely supplement your direct efforts at trigger recall with the second means available for identifying your triggers.

2. *The themes to triggers method.* Although they are displaced and therefore disguised, the narrative themes contained in a daydream narrative pool are responses to your triggers. They are, therefore, shaped by these triggers and must reflect the meanings of the trigger events that have evoked them.

Triggers and daydream themes are mirror images of each other.

Some of the themes in a narrative pool actually *describe in encoded form* the exact nature of a trigger event. These themes are called *bridging themes.* They are important clues to repressed triggers.

For example, the trigger of a job loss might be encoded in a story about a person who lost all of his or her money, or was locked out of an office. The trigger of a divorce might be encoded in a story about someone who runs away or who abandons another person.

Bridging themes are disguised clues to the trigger events.

Three additional points:

1. A definitive need to search for missing triggers is signalled when you have frame–related and power themes that cannot be accounted for by linking them to the triggers of which you are aware. In essence, *every powerful theme should be accounted for through an evident connection to a trigger event.* When this can't be done, you need to search for a fresh trigger or two.

2. In principle, psychological defenses attack triggers more than encoded themes.

Finding your triggers is one of the hardest parts of trigger decoding.

3. *Themes always tell the truth*—what they say through their encoded language is almost always the way things really are. Be sure, then, to satisfy or explain your themes through triggers whose qualities link to the disguised imagery.

Whenever you process and trigger decode a daydream, all of the most powerful and frame-related themes must be readily decodable in light of a trigger event that gives the themes a unified sense of meaning and intelligence.

Searching for Wendy's Triggers

Let's go back to the vignette with Wendy, explored in the previous chapter. To identify her triggers, we will need to know what she's gone through emotionally in the last few days. Triggers are specific events with distinctive meanings. They are not classes of events, general problems or broad issues, nor are they first and foremost our fantasies and inner worries.

Triggers are particular events with particular meanings; the search for triggers must be a search for specific emotionally charged events.

As I said, the search for triggers usually begins with efforts at direct recall. To allow the thematic pool to develop without bias, this search is undertaken after the first round of guided associating has been completed.

We will explore Wendy's direct trigger search in a moment. But before we do, we ourselves should turn to the themes to triggers method of searching for triggers to answer the following question.

Question 14.1

Review the themes in Wendy's entire daydream-associational network and use them to propose two possible trigger events to which she might well be adapting. That is, what might she be reacting to and who might be involved?

Answer 14.1

The main themes and people in Wendy's daydream network pertain to intruders, boyfriends, over-involvement with a mother (parent), separation anxiety, suicide attempt, unfaithful boyfriends, stealing, sister, injury, entrapment, having an affair, and break-up of the affair. These images suggest possible triggers involving problems with a boyfriend or an affair, some issue between Wendy and her mother and a sister, someone being unfaithful, an entrapping relationship, an issue with dishonesty, some kind of harmful incident, or some type of secured-frame/entrapment issue.

Each of these broad categories of themes speaks for a possible specific trigger event. For example, Wendy could have recently broken up with a boyfriend or he could have either left Wendy or become involved with another woman. Someone Wendy knows could have attempted suicide or done something else that was blatantly self-destructive, or someone could have been in an accident. Along different lines, Wendy's boyfriend could be pressing her to marry him, or her mother could be trying to prevent Wendy from living with him.

These are some of the possible triggers that would apply to this pool of themes—and there are many more related possibilities. Indeed, when Wendy gets around to her own themes to trigger search, this is exactly what she would do: get a sense of the general themes in her narrative pool and use them as her guide to identifying specific recent trigger events.

With this much said, it's time to turn to Wendy and her actual search for trigger events. Her first effort was to try to recall the most disturbing events of the past few days, especially those that had occurred most recently, earlier that day.

There had been some hurts at work, including a nasty call from a customer that had bothered her a lot. But probably the most disturbing incident had taken place during dinner with Walter. While Wendy couldn't quite put her finger on it, something about him was bothering her. She went through some of the details of their conversation during the meal and finally remembered that, over coffee, acting like he was revealing a guilty secret, Walter told her that he was going on a business trip with June, a woman in his office who had been seductive with Walter and whom Wendy felt Walter found attractive as well.

At their company's Christmas party last year, Wendy noticed that June was eating from Walter's plate. Wendy and Walter had argued about that incident, Wendy claiming that Walter had set it up and Walter claiming that Wendy was making something out of nothing. As is true of almost all conscious system arguments, neither of them had changed their minds and the issue eventually faded into the background of their relationship.

But the problem had sparked up again earlier this year when June showed up unexpectedly at Walter's apartment. Wendy and Walter were watching television when she appeared. June said she had some urgent business matters to go over with Walter and that she needed some crucial information to call a customer in Japan later that evening. The papers were confusing and only Walter could help her get them straightened out—which is what he did.

Once again, Wendy reacted to this encounter with suspicion, while Walter argued for the innocence of the incident. Wendy kept going back and forth in her mind, believing Walter one minute and thinking that he must be deceiving her the next. In typical conscious system fashion, she was unable to make up her mind as to what the truth really was.

Wendy next recalled that she never could understand what attracted Walter to June. She was a heavy-set, unattractive woman who liked to overeat. What could be so appealing about an unpredictable woman like that, Wendy wondered.

Wendy had raised her eyebrows when Walter mentioned the trip, but he was quick to reassure her that there was nothing to it. "My God," he added, "I'm not going to sleep with her, we're taking separate rooms, what do you want?"

The more Walter protested, the more Wendy wondered about what he was up to, but at the same time, she kept recriminating herself for being so suspicious and for not trusting him.

Trigger events are currently active, emotionally charged incidents that conjure up among its narrative associations a host of related past events. These consciously recalled incidents offer a historical perspective on the current trigger—as did the recollections given above for Wendy. She tried to rework these earlier incidents, in terms of their surface imagery, but her final conscious assessment was still uncertain—Walter might or might not be involved in some inappropriate way with June.

The conscious mind is seldom incisive. Even when a situation would be quite clear to a neutral observer, we tend to raise doubts that color our direct thinking and almost never allow us to settle on an unambiguous position. Conscious system processing of an emotionally charged trigger event is notoriously vague, uncertain, and often inclined to be self-hurtful in either its lack of resolve or its final decision. In contrast, deep unconscious processing is uncompromising, clear-headed, and accurate in its appraisals—which brings us back to realizing that we need to trigger decode our daydream images so we can make definitive and constructive decisions.

Wendy paused at this juncture to gather what she had generated and to try to organize her images—a self–observing effort that should be made from time to time whenever you process a daydream. She looked at the themes in her daydream network and juxtaposed them onto her known triggers, trying to match the thematic imagery with the meanings of the trigger event with Walter.

It was time to shift from her conscious reworking of this trigger to her unconscious assessment of the situation; time to get a second and more reliable opinion. Wendy had a rich pool of themes and an emotionally charged trigger.

She was now ready to link the themes to the trigger and let the themes speak to her as true perceptions and sound evaluations of the trigger event.

The Bridging Themes

There are two steps to this part of the process, *the linking of themes to triggers:*

1. Searching for bridging themes that connect the themes to the trigger event. The goal is to *find meanings in the thematic material that correspond to meanings in the trigger event—themes shared by each of them.* These connections provide convincing evidence that the daydream images are indeed a reflection of the unconscious processing of that particular trigger event.
2. Linking the themes to the trigger event and shaping the connection as decoded, valid perceptions of the actual, selectively perceived meanings of the triggering experience.

The specific goal Wendy set for herself here, then, was to allow her encoded images to speak to the trigger of Walter's going on a trip with June. To do this, she first had to convince herself that her daydream network did, indeed, reflect the working over of the triggering situation with Walter. She needed to find the bridging themes that linked her thematic pool with this trigger event.

Question 14.2

Rethink Wendy's daydream material and the nature of the trigger event with Walter—his announcement that he would be traveling with June. Identify as many <u>similar, shared, or bridging themes</u> in the two networks—the daydream material and the trigger event. When considering the trigger event side of the picture, you should include all of the direct, conscious associations that elaborated on the relationship between Walter and June—they are inherent to the triggering experience.

Answer 14.2

The following appear to be the main bridging themes, shared by both the thematic pool and the trigger event:

1. The theme of a business trip with a co-worker is found in the daydream network in the allusion to Della's (Wendy's sister's) business trip and it is found in the trigger event as well through Walter's plans to travel with June.

2. The theme of taking someone else's food appears in the daydream itself, and is connected to the trigger event in the memory of June eating from Walter's plate and to her tendency to overeat.

3. The unexpected appearance of an intruding party is found in the association to the daydream that alluded to Walter's mother's unexpected appearance at his apartment, and it emerges in the trigger network through the recollection of June's unexpected appearance at Walter's apartment.

4. A less definitive bridging image is seen in the daydream theme of a threesome (the engaged couple, and the woman the man became involved with) and in the threesome that is part of the trigger event (Walter, June, and Wendy).

There are, then, at least three or four strong themes that bridge the trigger event complex to the themes in Wendy's daydream network. She can, therefore, be quite confident that her imagery is, indeed, a reflection of her unconscious processing of this trigger event. The number and strength of the bridging themes indicates that the trigger has considerable emotional power and that Wendy has generated some very critical unconscious perceptions of Walter in light of his triggering announcement. A lot has been stirred up in Wendy and has been processed unconsciously—a lot that goes beyond her conscious view and uncertainties.

Bridging themes serve two functions:

1. Linking themes to triggers.

2. Introducing a measure of unconsciously perceived meaning into the decoding process. That is, these shared themes indicate aspects of the daydreamer's unconscious experience of the trigger event. Indeed, the linking of themes to triggers often begins with the meanings of the bridging themes and extends to the remainder of the network of themes.

To see how this works, let's move on to the next chapter in which Wendy's moment of deep insight materializes.

The Moment of Insight

Now that she knew her daydream stories contained her unconscious perceptions and of Walter's announcement, Wendy turned to the second step in the linking process—the linking of themes to triggers. Let's be clear now as to exactly how this connection of themes to triggers should be stated and understood.

The human mind reworks and adapts first and foremost to its environment—to impingements from others—and only second to its own reactions to those impingements. This means that the encoded themes in a daydream network reflect the actual nature of what has happened emotionally and reflect the best available solutions to the dilemmas and conflicts raised by these events. This tells us that the linking of themes to triggers should be accomplished in keeping with the following narrative model:

This is what happened (the trigger). . . this is what it means (the decoded perceptions). . . and this is what should be done about it (the decoded adaptive solutions).

The Trigger Decoded Narrative

Trigger decoding generates a story—a narrative picture of what really has happened as it was perceived subliminally and how it should be handled or adapted to. The essential communication in the linking/decoding moment is:

> *This is the story of what was experienced unconsciously and this is how it should be dealt with. In its simplest form, this is a cause-effect-solution tale of stimulus and response.*

Question 15.1

We know the trigger event Wendy is working over—Walter's planned trip with June. We have a large body of themes related to both frames and power. The themes reflect Wendy's unconscious perceptions of the trigger event—of Walter in light of the planned trip—and also encodes ways to respond to Walter, in light of what has been seen unconsciously.

Try as best you can to identify some of the unconscious perceptions and unconscious meanings that Wendy is experiencing in response to this trigger event. How is she perceiving what Walter is about to do? Is there consistency to these perceptions, and if so, what is it? How does Wendy's unconscious mind suggest that she deal with the situation—and with Walter?

Answer 15.1

Let's collect Wendy's unconscious perceptions in the sequence in which they emerged in her daydream and associations. The trigger is Walter's traveling with June. As you may have realized, the daydream itself encodes very little about the trigger event. The image of the woman taking something that belongs to Wendy (the cake, which encodes Walter) indicates that her unconscious perception is that June is taking Walter from her.

The flight taken by Wendy suggests a view of Walter running away from her. You should not be misled by the fact that the image alludes to Wendy herself and not to Walter. Remember that the realm of unconscious experience is a world where displacement is an essential part of communication—on this level, very little stands for itself. The trigger event serves as a guide to who is who. Thus, while, as we will see, the image of Wendy fleeing is, as you might have guessed, an encoded suggestion to how she should deal with Walter—get away from him—it is first and foremost an encoded perception of the trigger event, of Walter's flight from Wendy.

It is often said that everyone in a dream (and daydream) is part of the dreamer—a maxim that is, of course, a reflection of the old, inner mind/fantasy way of thinking without triggers. We can, however, extract a grain of truth from this statement and argue that everyone in a day dream is one or more other people—daydreams touch on a world of displaced and disguised, rather than direct, messages.

In this instance, Wendy's using herself to represent Walter is an excellent disguise because there is a natural tendency to sustain conscious system thinking in processing a daydream. The thought then would be that in referring to herself, Wendy must mean only herself—the encoded feature is lost. However, the principle is that this allusion is primarily saying something about Wendy's perceptions of the trigger event, and therefore of Walter, and only secondarily about herself—flight as her adaptive solution.

Through *condensation*, then, Wendy stands for both Walter and herself—for both a perception and a reaction to that perception. In this segment of the daydream, Wendy first reacts with anger at June's intrusion and Walter's complicity, and then flees from both. All in a single element of the daydream! The language/representational capacities of the human mind are quite amazing.

Wendy's associations to her daydream reveal a lot more about her unconscious processing of the trigger event than does the daydream itself. The first association, Walter's mother intruding on Wendy and him, speaks to the unconscious view of June as an unwelcome intruder into Wendy's relationship with Walter. The over-involvement between Walter and his mother speaks to a similar perception—June and Walter are enmeshed.

Notice first, that we now have a repetitive theme—a woman intruding into Wendy's life, specifically, into her relationship with Walter. Repetitive themes tend to support each other and lend strength to the decoded formulations you make of the encoded imagery.

Second, you can see again that the mechanism of *displacement* is at work. In order to process your daydreams, you must be able to think in terms of displacements.

Again—*in a daydream network, anyone can be someone else; determining who's who comes from using the trigger to shape the themes.*

In this story, Walter's mother stands for June, while for the moment Walter and Wendy stand for themselves. We know this is the case not by arbitrary guesses and assignments, but because the bridging themes, as they link to the trigger, tell us this must be the way the characters fall out.

Getting rid of Walter's mother is another encoded adaptive solution to the situation—a proposal that is rather different from Wendy's thoughts that she should flee the situation. Here, the adaptive recommendation is instead of Wendy running away, she should get rid of June. The story also again conveys the anger Wendy is feeling over what is happening.

Notice we now have clear evidence for our formulations in the consistency of the decoded images. While Wendy's conscious mind was waffling in its evaluation of the trigger event, her deep unconscious mind had but a single view of the situation—June and Walter are involved with each other and June is taking him away from Wendy.

We also can see that while consciously Wendy had no clear view of the trigger and no idea how to handle it, her unconscious mind had a precise view of the situation and suggested at least two different coping strategies.

The next story about Wendy's girlfriends and the mother who attempted suicide when her daughter moved away from her speaks for both Wendy's perception of loss—losing Walter—and her unconscious despair over the loss. This association alludes to a fiance who was involved sexually with other women—another encoded perception of Walter's unfaithfulness to Wendy. Here the recommended adaptive solution is to get out of the relationship—this time by getting rid of Walter.

Wendy's unconscious mind is not fantasizing or imagining this betrayal, but is perceiving the evidence for its actual existence.

The story about Della reiterates the theme of someone stealing from Wendy. Della clearly is a stand-in for June, and Walter is represented by Wendy's clothes. Notice Wendy's view of Walter as her cake and clothing, encoded images that reflect her view of her boyfriend in her unconscious mind, a view that bears further exploration. The deep unconscious mind has all kinds of information we can't get to directly, all of it greatly affecting our interactions with others and our inner state of mind.

The affair Wendy's sister had with her fellow worker again encodes Wendy's unconscious perception that Walter was involved sexually with June. The image of the ghost who caused an injury to Della also speaks for Wendy's unconscious perception that she is being injured by June—and by Walter (via condensation, the same person can represent both of them).

In trigger decoding this network of themes around the trigger of Walter's involvement with June, as unconsciously perceived by Wendy, we have repeatedly found that her unconscious view of the situation is that Walter was having an affair with June. The recommended coping strategies varied—Wendy should run away, break off the relationship with Walter, get Walter to end the relationship with June, harm herself, or attack and harm the two betrayers.

To summarize Wendy's decoded perceptions of the trigger event of Walter's going off with June, the highlights of the story can be condensed:

June has stolen Walter from me and Walter is lying when he says it isn't so. He's being unfaithful, self-destructive, hurtful, and deceitful. While I might try to get rid of June, the best solution to the situation is ending my relationship with Walter.

Encoded Validation

Given this decoded knowledge, of which Wendy had virtually no conscious awareness, how should she respond to the situation with Walter? That is, in principle, what should we do with the understanding we derive from trigger decoding efforts?

The answer is, first, we should unconsciously validate or confirm our initial trigger decoded impressions and, second, we should proceed with caution but pay careful attention to the perceptions, warning and advice emanating from our unconscious minds. The following is a sensible way to proceed:

1.   Take seriously your decoded unconscious perceptions, assessments, and coping strategies. If you have been careful with your trigger decoding, your decoded messages are very likely valid and invaluable.

2.   Because efforts to decode your daydream networks in light of their triggers must combat the conscious mind's defensiveness and preference for not knowing, you should always attempt to confirm your initial decoded impressions by freely turning to a fresh element of the original daydream and generating one or two new guided associations. Trigger decode these associations in light of the trigger in question and determine if the new images and themes validate your initial impressions.

Validation may take two forms:

a.   A fresh story that supports and adds new insights to the assessment you have already made. This is called cognitive validation because it adds meaning that confirms existing meanings.

b.   A story of someone wise, bright, effective, or otherwise functioning well—an encoded perception of the brilliance of your decoding effort. This is called personal validation because it confirms your insightfulness without adding fresh meanings to your understanding.

Be clear that *each of these forms of validation are encoded*—they are not direct statements, such as, "Wow, that really makes sense," or, "Oh sure, that's what that trigger event must have meant to me."

While a trigger decoded statement should make sense and be simple and logical, the confirmatory images must be found in a fresh story about something other than the trigger event and must be decoded to appreciate its confirming qualities.

Unconscious insights must be confirmed through encoded, unconscious messages.

3. Use your freshly won understanding cautiously and wisely. You have discovered things you were not able to perceive consciously but could see unconsciously. You have gained knowledge that your mind is designed not to be aware of painful insights that can help you better manage your life. An advisable attitude is one of humility and appreciation that we all have our encoded secrets and that decoding brings with it painful but necessary comprehension.

Be especially careful about imparting your insights to others. Often, your perceptions touch on things other people do not and wish not to know about themselves—things they would deny if you confronted them. The best course is to observe other people and yourself very carefully, using your newly achieved unconscious wisdom as your guide. If you are right about what's going on, you will be surprised at how many clues your conscious mind had previously missed and can now see.

When the supplementary conscious evidence becomes sufficiently clear, you can, with the support of unconscious confirmation, confidently act on the basis of your new insights—either diplomatically confronting or otherwise dealing with the other person(s) or deciding to get out of a hurtful relationship. The decision is yours, best made after discussing the issues with the other party, but carried out with the confidence that comes from using your unconscious intelligence as your guide.

4. Because you can carry out trigger decoding only with your conscious mind, and this part of your mind is so defensively oriented, *be prepared to reformulate your thinking whenever encoded validation fails to materialize or the slightest sign of doubt appears.* Be sure to

trigger decode your next day's daydream network to validate today's decoded formulations. When the situation is serious, check and recheck your decoding efforts for as many days as necessary. Trigger decoding is a valuable tool, but it needs to be used judiciously.

Wendy's Efforts at Validation

To finish this part of Wendy's story, she decided to generate a fresh guided association to her daydream to see if decoding her new story would or would not validate her interpretation of her previous images. Her thoughts went to the coffee bar, which now brought to mind a recent meeting with her friend Anne in a coffee bar. Anne had been married and was badly hurt when her husband got involved with another woman. Anne blamed herself for the hurt because she knew she never should have married a man who was known for his many affairs—she was not the first woman he had suddenly deserted. "Be careful who you get involved with," she had warned Wendy, adding "that once things turned sour, the thing to do is get out because they won't get better."

Question 15.2

Is this fresh story confirmation of Wendy's prior trigger decoding efforts? If so, what is the nature of the validation? If not, why not? Also, does this story suggest another yet unnoticed aspect to the situation between Wendy and Walter, and if so, what is it?

Answer 15.2

This fresh guided association does indeed confirm Wendy's trigger decoded formulations of her unconscious perceptions of the situation with Walter. It does so through a fresh story of betrayal. But also it adds a dimension to the situation that had not been previously developed. The idea that Anne should have known what her husband was like reminded Wendy that the friend who had introduced Wendy to

Walter had warned Wendy that Walter had a history of being easily distracted from his commitments to women.

Wendy had consciously chosen to ignore this warning, partly because unconsciously she was still suffering from guilt over having betrayed her previous boyfriend. We are all quite adept at arranging our own punishments for deeds we all too quickly dismiss consciously and allow to simmer in our unconscious minds.

In this new story, the advised coping strategy is that Wendy should drop Walter—he's not going to change. This decision, which seems quite wise, was not one that Wendy could have made based on her conscious thinking alone.

One other point. Oddly enough, the association to Anne brought back a vivid daydream that Wendy had after her first date with Walter. Wendy couldn't remember all of it, but she did recall there was an image of a threesome—a woman, herself, and Walter. Wendy realized her daydream encoded her deeply unconscious appreciation of Walter's tendency for betrayal—the very thing her conscious mind had ignored and denied. Wendy's failure to trigger decode this daydream warning should serve as a warning to all of us—trigger decode your daydreams or suffer the consequences of ignorance and the need for self-harm.

Soon after processing this daydream, Wendy was able to collect a surprisingly large number of clues to Walter's infidelity, so by the time she confronted him with the evidence, Walter confessed to his infidelity. Despite Walter's pleas that he would stop seeing June and that he wanted things to work out with Wendy, she heeded her own unconscious warning that Walter really wouldn't change and broke off her relationship with him at that very moment.

Wendy processed her daydreams that night and again found validation for her unconscious perceptions and conscious decision. An image of being able to fly a small airplane, of being free and soaring, and a story about a girlfriend who broke up with an unfaithful boyfriend and soon found "Mr. Right" and eventually got married, were among the encoded associations that told Wendy she had made the right decision. She also felt better emotionally than she had in months—taking her own unconscious advice brought her a measure of temporary pain, but with it, a lot of good things on many levels.

Processing our daydreams takes effort, must be carried out in the face of subtle and gross resistances, and brings us to compelling and vital realizations that also are a shock to our emotional equilibrium. Nevertheless, if you want to negotiate your emotional life more effectively, to be far more content and far less self-hurtful, there's no better way to accomplish it. Life is tough, solving its emotional ills is tough, and so is trigger decoding your daydreams. But it takes tough, solution to handle the tough courses of our lives.

Exercise 15.1

To close this chapter, take your most recent daydreams, engage in guided associating to their elements, carry out a trigger search, and link your most compelling trigger event to your pool of themes. In doing this exercise, list in your mind the main components of the process that you are carrying out—what are the essentials of trigger decoding?

Comment 15.1

In practicing your trigger decoding of a daydream, these are the essentials you should be sure to include in your effort:

1. Begin with one or more daydreams. It is promising but not essential for the process if the surface imagery has some power.
2. Do your guided associating to the daydream, making sure you generate narratives, associate to the strongest elements of the daydream imagery, and create both power themes and frame allusions.
3. Search for and discover your most powerfully active trigger events using both direct recall and themes as clues to triggers.
4. Link the themes to the key trigger, telling a story of stimulus and response, event and unconscious experience—and coping strategies.

That's trigger decoding in the proverbial nutshell. To see that it all happens as it should, let's move on to the final chapter and deal with the important issue of repressed or missing trigger events.

CHAPTER 16

Searching for Hidden Triggers

We have one important task left to consider before completing our explorations of the surface and depth of daydreams. We need to deal with the defensive preferences of the conscious mind that lead us automatically to *repress many significant trigger events,* especially while we are processing our daydreams. Indeed, it is not uncommon to discover that the most crucial trigger or the most important meanings of a known trigger event has been subjected to repression. A full and effective knowledge of ourselves and our unconscious experiences is possible only when we become adept at unearthing these missing trigger events so we can process their unconscious meanings.

In the previous chapter, I pointed out that there are two ways to search for and discover missing triggers: first, through direct efforts at recall and, second, by using the themes in your daydream network as clues to your more repressed trigger events. Both methods must be used assiduously to ensure that you capture as many of your triggers as possible.

Wendy's Search for a Hidden Trigger

Let's return one last time to Wendy and her daydream network, to see how she arrived at searching for and discovering a critical repressed trigger event she had been reworking through *condensation,* with the same network of images and themes that had reflected her unconscious processing of the trigger event with Walter. As we will see, in many ways this trigger was possibly even more important to Wendy than her known trigger—which often is the case.

Having processed the situation with Walter to her satisfaction, Wendy still felt uneasy. Something else was bothering her, but she couldn't decide what it was. She also was disturbed by the image of the attempted suicide. It was a strong theme that seemed to be unrelated to the trigger involving Walter. Wendy was certain she did not feel suicidal about breaking up with him—in fact, in many ways it was a relief. The suicide image needed a trigger—there was something more Wendy was working over and she wanted to know what it was.

As noted, any indication of unfinished processing should evoke a search for missing triggers. Every powerful image in a daydream network should be meaningfully linked to a trigger event—if not, there must be a missing trigger that would provide the connection.

Wendy searched through the incidents of her day for a strong trigger she hadn't yet brought into focus. She thought of a run-in with a fellow employee, some grief with the waitress at the restaurant where she had lunch, and several other incidents, but none seemed very strong. Why then was she still so tense?

With direct recall failing her, Wendy turned to her daydream network. She reviewed the themes with an ear for how they might bridge over, and be clues to, the repressed trigger for which she was searching. Coffee bar, a couple taking food from her, sex with someone, an intrusive mother, girlfriends living together, a philanderer, her sister stealing clothing from her, having an affair, getting injured. Wendy abstracted her themes and tried to allow them to jar her memory. The mother theme had come up twice, but her mother hadn't called her that day. What was she missing?

Wendy now noticed that in her summary, she had bypassed the strong image that had made her feel that she had missed a critical trigger—the mother who had attempted suicide when her daughter left home. Suddenly, the missing trigger was in the forefront of Wendy's mind—how could she have forgotten it?

Sylvia, one of Wendy's two women friends who were sharing an apartment, had called her at work that day. Wendy was busy and could talk only for a minute or two, long enough for Sylvia to mention that Alicia was moving out of their apartment to live with her new boyfriend. There would be an opportunity for Wendy to move in with Sylvia if she wanted to. We'll talk about it later, Wendy had said, abruptly breaking off the conversation seemingly because she had so much work to do.

Here was another strong trigger event, which had been repressed despite the manifest allusions to Sylvia and Alicia in Wendy's processing of her daydream—another tribute to the repressive powers of the conscious mind. Our minds obliterate emotional issues of high intensity every day of our lives and without trigger decoding, we have no idea what's happening.

What about this trigger? Why did Wendy repress it? Manifestly, Sylvia was offering Wendy a chance to move out of her house where she still lived with her parents. However, this is the kind of trigger certain to be overloaded with implications—some of them will be picked up consciously, but many will be processed outside of awareness and will need to be trigger decoded.

Wendy and Sylvia had previously discussed the possibility that Alicia would move out of the apartment she shared with Sylvia. So Wendy knew it was coming (keep in mind the themes from her daydream network as we go through this exercise—here, the theme is knowing something would happen). They also had spoken of the possibility that Wendy would move out of her parents' home and live with Sylvia if that were to occur. It was a prospect Wendy consciously welcomed, yet she had a lot of conflict about it—small wonder she had repressed the trigger. The telephone call from Sylvia announced a moment of truth for Wendy—to leave home or to not leave home, that was the question.

Consciously, as soon as she hung up the telephone, Wendy had reimmersed herself in her work and dropped the subject entirely. She hadn't thought of it again until it returned during her trigger search,

Now that she began to mull it over, her first thought was that she didn't earn enough money to live outside of her parents' home. Besides, Sylvia wasn't an easy person to get along with and the move would mean Wendy would have to travel a long distance from the apartment to get to work. Consciously, moving didn't seem all that attractive. On the other hand, getting away from her parents, and especially from her mother, sounded like a great idea. Her mother was a meddling, controlling woman who hounded Wendy much of the time.

Despite the evident advantages, Wendy felt consciously inclined to turn down Sylvia's offer of the apartment. But she hated giving up a chance to be on her own. Once again, Wendy was caught up in a conscious system exploration of an emotionally charged trigger event and decision, and she could not make a definitive choice. She decided to turn to her deep unconscious system and to trigger decode her daydream network in light of this new trigger situation. Wendy had every reason to expect that an optimal solution to her conflict would materialize from these efforts.

Question 16.1

As best you can, identify the main bridging themes that connect the daydream network with this trigger event and its implications or meanings. Do as much trigger decoding as you can by linking the themes to the trigger. What does Wendy's deep unconscious mind seem to be telling her to do about the offer of the apartment?

Answer 16.1

We'll take our answer from Wendy. She began her processing with the bridging theme she had missed earlier—the allusions to the apartment and to Sylvia and Alicia. She also noticed a few other bridging images—intrusive women and mothers, shared spaces, and a nice neighborhood.

Wendy decided to be less systematic with her efforts at linking this time and allowed her mind to drift over the stories and themes in her daydream network, and to trigger decode them as she went along. She thought first of her favorable view of the neighborhood where the apartment was located. In her daydream, she escaped the coffee bar, which must represent her home (she usually has coffee with her mother in the morning and sometimes her father joins them), and went out to the safe brightness of a beautiful part of the city.

The decoded message appeared to be: Your mother is intrusive and invades your space (eating the cake) and your father doesn't protect you. Get out of your home and move into the beautiful, liberating apartment.

The decoded message from her deep unconscious wisdom system seems clear and runs counter to Wendy's conscious inclination to stay at home.

The unfaithful man brings to mind Wendy's suspicion that her parents have been quarreling because her father is having an affair with another woman. Wendy doesn't like being home, hearing them go at it; getting away would be a relief. Wendy's mother insists that Wendy pay for her room and board, but she often asks for more money than she's entitled to—it's like the image of her sister who stole from her. Again, the situation at home is cast in a negative light.

At this point, Wendy realized she's avoided several powerful images and themes—another conscious system, defensive tendency. The suicide attempt of Alicia's mother prompted Wendy to recall that once, when Della wanted to move out of the family house, their mother got hysterical, said Della didn't care what happened to her, and said she might as well end her life at that very moment. Della stayed on, but soon became physically ill and suffered emotionally until she finally left home—and her mother accepted the move and survived quite nicely.

More and more, Wendy's deep unconscious mind seemed to be telling her to leave home like her sister had done. It was time to detach from her smothering mother as she had felt Walter should do with his mother—this was her deeply unconscious advice to herself. The stories indicated her mother might object, but would handle it quite well—as would Wendy. In fact, Wendy realized that her concerns about how her mother would respond to the move were displaced from herself—she was worried about having her independence and coping with her newfound freedom.

Somehow this brought Wendy back to Della and this time she thought about her sister getting trapped in the elevator. Sylvia's apartment was on the fifth floor of an elevator building. Moving into the apartment would be securing a frame in Wendy's life—a woman in her late 20s who still lives at home is in a frame-deviant situation. Wendy's conscious mind didn't think of it that way, but her unconscious mind certainly did—this realization is encoded in the closed space represented by the elevator.

Securing the frame would give Wendy her freedom and a chance to meet a new man, but it also was seen as dangerously entrapping—the image of Della trapped in the elevator and getting panicky encoded Wendy's own secured frame fears. The images of being reassured and then rescued reflected Wendy's realization that she could master these anxieties. Nevertheless, these anxieties must have been a strong unconscious factor in her reluctance to move.

Wendy now stepped back to self-observe—to see what her decoding efforts had produced. She recognized her secured-frame anxieties and her own enmeshment with her mother, whom she feared leaving. The adaptive solution of her deep unconscious mind was unmistakable and appeared in several forms. The clearest encoded statement of this solution seemed to be encoded in the story of Walter and his mother—decoded, it said Wendy was too enmeshed with her mother and should get away from her. It was clear to Wendy that she had to overcome her secured-frame anxieties and move into the apartment as soon as Alicia left.

Had Wendy made this decision based on her conscious intelligence and reasoning, she would have coped with the trigger event by turning down Sylvia's offer. Through trigger decoding, Wendy arrived at the very opposite decision, a far healthier and adaptive solution at that.

The positive side of accepting Sylvia's offer was confirmed when Wendy turned to develop one last association to her daydream. This time her mind went to the cake which prompted her to remember that

Sylvia loves to bake. Wendy recalled a time when Sylvia had invited her to what turned out to be an elegant dinner at her apartment. The satisfying qualities of the image were unmistakable and the themes served to confirm the decision Wendy had finally made—to make the move. In time, that's exactly what happened and it's all going very well for Wendy. Oddly enough, she's also never had a better relationship with her mother.

Some Final Thoughts

In searching for deep unconscious meaning and wisdom, you have two tasks. The first is the easier of the two—remembering your daydreams or making up a few imaginary stories for immediate processing. This is the *encoded theme* part of the process and everyone can learn to generate a thematic pool. With effort, every thematic pool can be provided with associated stories that ensure you have both power and frame-related themes ready for the linking process. While some networks will, of course, be stronger and more meaningful than others, the theme part of this process is easily fulfilled.

The second part of the process is *identifying your key triggers*. It is here that conscious system defenses are strongest. It is amazing to see how much repression can be directed at the recall of critical trigger events. It is, therefore, imperative to appreciate the indications of a missing trigger so you know you must look further. In essence, they are:

1. If you can find only one trigger event to process, you can be sure there are other triggers in need of identification and reworking.
2. If there are power and frame-related themes that have not been accounted for by the known triggers, there are unknown triggers in need of discovery.
3. If there appear to be bridging themes that hint at a missing trigger, one is missing for sure.
4. If validation of your linking efforts does not materialize, this means there's another trigger you have missed—one that would better fit the themes and allow for encoded confirmation of the fresh linking effort.

5. If you feel uncomfortable and dissatisfied with your decoding efforts, there probably is another trigger in need of processing.

6. If the linking effort produced fairly obvious meanings that lacked surprise, chances are there's another trigger for which linking will generate unexpected insights.

7. If you still are disturbed in any way or suffering from an emotional symptom, or if you still are unclear about an emotionally charged decision, then you are probably missing a key trigger event.

A wise principle states that it is advisable to never be complacent about identified triggers. Unless an overwhelming trauma is at hand, the chances are great that you will automatically miss some important trigger events that need to be pursued until rescued from repression.

Once you begin to play with and process your daydreams, you will see for yourself that daydreams rather than dreams are the human mind's most inventive, useful, and potentially healing creations. As a form of play, their creative denial and healing qualities are a supreme gift. As a form of direct communication, they tell us a great deal about the surface of our emotional lives. And as a type of encoded message, they embody a deeply unconscious intelligence that is unmatched in the emotional realm.

Processing a daydream a day helps keep the medical doctor and psychotherapist away—to say nothing about the quality of life it can provide. It is my fervent hope that this book has cleared a path to that very effort. I wish you all the best in pursuing that rewarding pathway—don't give up on it, ever!

Index